ORGANIC PARENTING

The **Prevention** of

PARENT DEFICIT DISORDER

By Koko Preston, MA

BOOK PUBLISHERS NETWORK

Book Publishers Network
P.O. Box 2256
Bothell • WA • 98041
PH • 425-483-3040
www.bookpublishersnetwork.com

10 9 8 7 6 5 4 3 2 1

Printed in the United States of America

LCCN 2008941096
ISBN10 1-935359-03-7
ISBN13 978-1-935359-03-6

Editor: Julie Scandora
Cover Designer: Laura Zugzda
Typographer: Stephanie Martindale

For my children
Tom
Nancy
Elizabeth
Emily
Diane
&

my grandchildren
Devon
Cabot
&
those of you who yet are unborn …

to be close to you …

This is the earnest work. Each of us given
only so many mornings to do it —
to look around and love.

~Mary Oliver, "The Deer"

Contents

Preface

All things are interconnected.
Everything goes somewhere.
There's no such thing as a free lunch.
Nature bats last.

~Ernest Callenbach
Ecology

The most important lesson nature requires us to learn is nurturing.

More than thirty years ago my family lived next to a house rented for the summer to a clan consisting of a grandmother, mother, and several children. The father worked in the city and returned to his family in the country on weekends. My young son was fascinated by the children playing and would take my hand and lead me along the wooded path that connected our backyards. One day the crone, or grandmother, told me never to say "don't" to my son.

Now, I had never thought about the word "don't" before, but I realized that she was right. "Don't" is negating and makes us feel bad, just the opposite of what I wanted to convey to my beautiful little boy, who was so trusting and honorable. I learned two valuable lessons that summer so long ago: to direct positively and encouragingly; and the value of advice received from someone who is experienced. Now I am the Crone, and it is my responsibility to teach those who want to learn.

I work part-time at the Maine Lighthouse Museum (MLM) in Rockland, Maine. The MLM offers wonderful Saturday afternoon programs free to the public. One Saturday, a couple who served as lighthouse keepers — a gentleman who served in the Coast Guard and his wife — presented. They raised six children and have been married for fifty-five years. The woman said that she kept a perfect keeper's house and believed that to do so was her job. But now she realizes that her children were what was most important. I have been wanting to write a book about raising children, and I wonder if I was meant to hear this good woman's lament.

Raising our children is the most important work most of us will ever do. Our whole existence should model healthy behavior for our children. Every decision we make should be in the best interests of our children. Then children will know and understand that they are cherished. They will feel good about themselves and be able to love and to live well.

When you know how and when you are doing it right, parenting is easy and a joy. It is only hard going when you are on the wrong path. And it is unfair to expect you to know the right path without a map.

You are flying a plane, and you have a destination. You understand that the plane will be blown off course, and as the pilot, you will have to correct its course. If you are distracted by a detour, it may take you longer to get to your destination. Even if you plan and prepare carefully, you might run out of fuel or meet an unexpected storm. You might become ill during a flight. Circumstances can inhibit or prohibit your ultimate arrival. Every journey taken is different. As a parent, you have the destination of raising a whole child. And it helps to know where you are going and to plan and prepare for your journey so you can make the necessary adjustments as you fly with your child.

It helps to have a standard to guide us and to remind us of what our purpose is and to show us the way because sometimes when we are in conflict, *the way* is not clear. There are so many confusing distractions. It may not appear to be that simple and we can get stuck or paralyzed. Standards, rules, and maps do not have to govern us but to serve us as a guide to break down what appears to be impossibly complex into a simpler, manageable task. Simplicity helps us to do what we want and have to do: to raise beautiful children as nature intends for us to do. And, in turn, our children will make the world a more beautiful place.

Organic parenting is an approach or a style of parenting rather than a strict set of rules that is right for all children of every temperament, personality, age and stage, or physical, mental, emotional, and spiritual condition. Organic parenting is responsive parenting tailored to meet each child at his or her point of need and is consistently flexible. The information and advice I offer you applies to all children everywhere, anytime.

Like Johnny Appleseed, I plant seeds of empathy. I hope this book will be useful and helpful to you.

About Parent Deficit Disorder

This book introduces what I call Parent Deficit Disorder. Also, Mother Deficit Disorder, Father Deficit Disorder, Nurture Deficit Disorder. All are facets of a prevalent cause of much unnecessary suffering, of disconnected people, of the current epidemic of deadening and deadly detachment. The antidote is *organic parenting*. Prevention through education is key. Parents are the solution — parents giving children the *family* they need.

Cover Story: Roots and Wings

> *"Good parents give their children* Roots and Wings. Roots *to know where home is,* Wings *to fly away and exercise what's been taught them."*
>
> ~ Jonas Salk (1914-1995)

Jonas Salk was born in New York City to Russian-Jewish immigrants who had no formal education but encouraged their children to succeed. Mr. Salk was fascinated by medical science and attended medical school. Hailed as a "miracle worker," after many years of painstaking research, Mr. Salk developed the vaccine against poliomyelitis, epidemic in the summertime of the 1950's, thus lifting the very real fear of this crippling and sometimes fatal viral infection forever. Mr. Salk refused to patent the vaccine. "He had no desire to profit personally from the discovery, but merely wished to see the vaccine disseminated as widely as possible." Mr. Salk learned his values of Roots and Wings from his parents. And he passed these values of deep roots to ground us and expansive wings to soar on to his sons. His sons also became medical scientists. In his last years, Mr. Salk and his sons collaborated to find a vaccine against AIDS. Each generation followed their own parents' examples, guiding their children in life.

A good mother I know told me that when she sees the front cover of this book, she thinks of *Roots and Wings*. I can see what she means.

Acknowledgments

It is customary to give thanks to those who have helped us. Every person has a story. I learn from your stories. If you know me, then you have contributed to the making of this manuscript. I am grateful to have learned from each one of you. Thank you!

I am deeply grateful to have a husband who "gets it" 100 percent. It is my husband, Dale, who coined the phrase *Organic Parenting*.

I want to give particular thanks to Pamela Benner. Pamela read my manuscript with a meticulous eye and an embracing heart. I greatly value and have incorporated her helpful suggestions. Of course, any shortcomings in *Organic Parenting* are my own responsibility.

No one can realistically expect to undertake a major project such as completing a book alone. The process of publishing a book requires the support of others who are experts in their fields. Without Sheryn Hara of Book Publishers Network (BPN) and the good folks that work with her, my manuscript could never have evolved into a book. Much deserved credit goes to Laura Zugzda who composed the delightful cover, Stephanie

Martindale who intuitively arranged the interior design, and editor Julie Scandora for her respectful review of my words for clarity and integrity. Words are powerful. A publisher whose mission is "changing the world one book at a time" makes it possible to exercise this power, making these words available to so many others who might benefit. Thank you all!

While this book strives to focus on what is healthy and positive, it is born of — is in response to — the pain I have witnessed in those whom I love and care about. I have learned profound lessons in my attempt to make sense of their suffering. These folks are the true authors of this book. I am but the messenger.

There are some special folks who are close to me. You make my life worth living. And I am so glad that you exist!

Introduction

I have written this book and discarded it to begin over a dozen times. I was never satisfied with what I had written. Last night my wise and wonderful daughter advised me not to be too critical. I am telling you this story to encourage you not to be too critical of yourself. Be as forgiving with yourself as you would with others. If you insist upon perfection you will set yourself up for failure. Your child neither needs nor expects you to be a "perfect" parent, but you can be perfectly acceptable. Do what you can. You can be good enough.

The core of every child is love. The true self is good. We have to express who we are. Bad behavior is within our nature but it is not our nature. Bad behavior is in reaction to and the expression of good, frustrated and denied. We all are divine. Some of us just don't know it.

The vicious behavior of a rabid animal is the disease talking. When people behave badly it is the disease talking. It is normal, natural, and healthy to be good. Abraham Maslow devoted his life to the study of health and goodness which walk hand-in-hand.

> *The fact is that people are good, if only their fundamental wishes are satisfied, their wish for affection and security. Give people affection and security, and they will give affection and be secure in their feelings and their behavior.*
>
> ~ Abraham Maslow

Trust in the essential goodness of your child *and yourself.* Parent by the brain in your heart.

We do not need more and more distancing technology which has already run amok and distances human beings from life, from one another, costly and time-consuming research and data (with "measurable" results likely based upon flawed research), more statistics (which can be manipulated), the hypocrisy of political correctness, the corruption of cultural garbage, the pretentious posturing of professional or academic jargon, strategies fostering convenience, or methods of controlling and managing children. All of these things get in the way of our being human, authentic and connected. They contribute to the cause of unnecessary suffering.

To be connected is to be healthy and intact. To bleed is normal and healthy when skin is cut, but is a cut normal and healthy? Intact skin is normal and desirable, as are intact (connected), healthy children — children who have an abundant capacity for trust, empathy and genuine affection. These qualities define what it is to be human.

Children Are Like Flowers

A dear friend once gave me a gift of four paperwhite bulbs with a glass container and stones. I was delighted with her gift. Just her thoughtfulness and effort and the delicate beauty and fragrance of the flowers during the dead of winter would have been enough. But her gift was ultimately much more than that. I learned a lesson!

For years I had planted paperwhites. Each time I had placed the bulbs in shallow bowls, and for years I had been dismayed that the stalks toppled over every time, that I did not know how to support them, and that they lost their bloom too soon.

The container my friend gave me was a tall glass cylinder and the stones half filled the container. When the bulbs were placed on top of the stones, there was ample space for the long roots to gain a secure foothold. Because the roots were anchored, the stalks remained upright. For the first time, my paper whites did not go bottoms-up. And because they were a special gift, I placed them in my office where I could see them regularly and for long stretches and inhale their heady fragrance while I typed. Since my office is *cooler* than my living room, the blossoms lasted longer.

Now, placing the bulbs in a taller planter that provided ample space to accommodate long roots seems like common sense. Yet, I never thought of it! I love learning how to do better!

Before learning this lesson, I had done the same thing over and over, getting the same results. It is a matter of cause and effect. If I do this, then that will happen. I have to change what I do if I want a different result. We cannot know what we do not know. When we know better, we do better.

Only a few years ago, I realized that the cultivation of flowers is a good metaphor for the cultivation of children. Plants are good teachers. I am aware of two differences between raising plants and children:

- One, a plant is "just" a plant. It's not a big deal if we goof. Unlike a child, a plant is not our priority. In a healthy culture and society, adults pay heartservice that children are *the* priority.

- Two, the level of emotionality is less when caring for flowers. Rather than feeling and reacting defensively, we gratefully accept helpful advice about caring for our houseplants or gardens.

The leaves on my geraniums were turning increasingly yellow. So I gave them increasingly more water believing that was what they needed. Finally, I learned from a more experienced geranium grower that the leaves were yellowing because I was *over*watering them! Geraniums like to be dry before they are given a nice deep watering.

I *love* getting advice from veteran gardeners because I WANT to take good care of my geraniums, but I don't always know how. I choose which advice fits me and my situation. Listening to advice can help me avoid unnecessary regrets and remorse. I learn from experience and become a better gardener with each passing year. Personal experience is the most powerful of teachers when we pay attention to the right lessons. Unless I listen to the advice of others, I cannot avoid pitfalls I don't know about. And I would have and could have avoided them, *if only I had known.*

Like all living things, flowers want to be loved. I show my plants my love for them by the care I give them. I take care of them by giving them what they need to be healthy. I have learned an absolute in this age of relativism: *Nature requires nurturing.* Nature requires nurturing species-specific. Nurturing is biologically determined. Kittens need the care that mama cats can give. Ducklings need mama ducks. Humans need human mothers. The nature versus nurture debate is bogus. Nurturing is inherent in nature. Flowers and humans are elements of nature.

Caring for my houseplants and backyard garden has taught me:

- Within every humble seed is a miracle! The Alpine strawberry seed is a speck. But the right environment gives amazing life to that speck.

- Geraniums need my time and attention. It does not matter what the reason might be for my neglect: Inconvenience, too little time, ignorance, lack of funds, the results are the same — a sad plant that does poorly. I can see the healthy difference when I take care of my plants. It is as if they say, "Thank you!"

- Geraniums need nourishment such as air, soil, water, and light. I have to be sensitive to and responsive to their individual and changing needs. *It is my responsiveness that has to be consistent.* I have to be attuned to my plant's needs — to be one with my plants.

- Flowers need protection from pests, predators, and abuse such as trampling. My eggplants and zinnias cannot protect themselves against ravaging Japanese beetles. Certainly, plants develop some degree of defense. Still, plants are vulnerable and defenseless against neglect or attack. If they depend on my care, I have to be vigilant for them.

- Geraniums and tomato plants need support and guidance. They have to be staked early in their development, or they will grow bent and crooked. If I try to straighten them, I may be too late, and they will break.

- Seedlings are fragile and have to be handled tenderly to avoid causing damage from which they may not recover. The younger the plant, the more vulnerable. The needs of younger plants are more immediate. I have to be present, mindful, connected when working with living things.

- A more mature, stronger, and healthy plant can endure deprivation with less urgency, though there is a limit. And beyond that line there can be no return. The damage can be permanent.

- Flowers are fleeting. Exquisitely delicate coral pink poppy petals bloom one day, and then they are gone. I want to be there to see them when they bloom because they go around only once.

- Plants grow according to nature's timetable, not mine. Providing optimal growing conditions works. Attempting to hurry or force a plant to grow results in distortion.

- "Forcing" bulbs indoors during winter might be termed "coaxing." Recently, I have learned that there can be a price for this conditioning. Often, forced bulbs have used so much energy to grow out of season that they are spent and will not bloom another time. We can condition a plant to grow against nature, but there is always a price.

- Seeds have a much better chance of germinating and growing into strong and healthy flowers and vegetables when I follow the planting instructions, and pay attention to the warnings and recommendations on the back of the seed packet. For best results, I have learned to read and follow the directions.

- By their behavior, my plants tell me if they are getting what they need and that I am doing what I should be doing: healthy or unhealthy, strong and beautiful or sickly, happy or sad.

- For a plant to benefit from watering, the soil has to be loose and soft. Water rolls off and around soil that is hard or too dry. I have to till the earth and water consistently, gently, gradually so the dirt can absorb the moisture — so the soil can be open to receive my offering.

- Rampant and bullying weeds can threaten to surround and deprive fledgling flowers and vegetables of necessary nutrients and take over the garden. I have to weed diligently if I want my young plants to thrive.

- Be patient. I have wondered if the green shoots of a tulip or amaryllis bulb would make an appearance. Simply, some bulbs are "late bloomers." A sprig in spring will grow into a bush by the end of the growing season. If I give up on a bulb or twig too soon, I might miss out on the gifts they have to offer.

- When I take care of my geraniums I get attached to them. The more I take care of them, the more I care about them. The more I care about them the more I want to take care of them. Fascinating, isn't it?

- My garden nourishes me! I love my flowers! They bring a smile to my face. I get up in the morning looking forward to their daily changes. I need my flowers.

Can you see how these lessons on caring for plants can be applied to caring for children? Can you add an observation of your own?

After a heavy night rain, I discovered the following morning that my delphiniums had been severed almost in two at the point where I had tied the tall stalks to the stakes. I learned from that experience to provide support for those gorgeous blue blooms higher up as well as lower down.

Reinventing the wheel can be a dangerous approach to raising children. Trial and error might be okay for growing plants, but for children the price can be too high. We do not want to sever our children in two — an injury from which they might never recover. When the environment is right — and for infants and small children the mother *is* the environment — then a child can grow straight and tall and beautiful. Just as nature intended a child to grow. Just like delphiniums.

Flower and vegetable seeds have instructions on the back of the packet that are clear, simple, and direct. The information and advice are based upon years of experience and observation. Experts tell us what is good for a plant and what works. You can read this book on raising children as you would the directions on the back of a seed packet.

And as you read, *please* remember that this instruction book on raising children is not at all about finding fault and pointing blame. Rather, it provides an opportunity for exploration and discovery. It serves as a reminder to be mindful of the link between cause and effect. Just as you must understand how much water each plant needs to thrive, you must be aware of what children need to flourish. Attend to them well, and you will grow *connected* children.

Parent Deficit Disorder: What Is Happening and Why

We are in a time of social crisis: We are suffering an epidemic as threatening to our well-being as that of smallpox or polio. A parental vacuum is the pathogen leading to the epidemic of the contagion of deadening and deadly detachment. Detachment also can be referred to as disconnection or the many diseases of non-attachment. Detachment is the umbrella for most mental and much physical illness. People who are disconnected do not care. And a society that has ceased to care is dangerous. We are collectively committing suicide. While there is no cure for detachment, it is preventable. The origin of most mental illness and many physical illnesses can be found in infancy and early childhood.

A motherless child is the essence of detachment. To be detached is to be condemned in infancy to an eternal state of Post Traumatic Stress Disorder (PTSD) for which there can be little comfort. We homo sapiens are social animals. To be detached is to be condemned for life to a prison sentence of isolation and dissociation, in which your heart can feel no love. To feel no love is the worst disease a human being can suffer. Our prisons are filled with detached people who know only violence and rejection, who can feel no love.

We can protect our children from devastating disconnection with the most amazing thing in the world. You can inoculate your child by practicing *organic parenting* also known as attachment parenting. Other terms to describe this style of parenting are connected parenting, empathic parenting, natural parenting, intuitive parenting, responsive parenting, ecological parenting, and, for infants under one year, in-arms parenting.

Parenting, beginning with mothering and then fathering, is the single most important factor influencing a child's life. Mothering is not the only thing, but it is necessary. Without mothering the rest does not matter. Once the need for mothering has been met, fathering has to be present for balance and wholeness. Mother Earth and Father Sky. Nurturer and Teacher. Both are necessary.

Organic or attachment parenting is based upon *trust*. You trust that your baby will learn and grow. Your baby trusts that you will give him the care he needs to learn and grow. Each trusts in the other's innate goodness.

More than anything else in the world your child wants to be close to you. It is that sense of closeness with self, others, and nature that makes life worth living. The pattern of connection that begins in the womb is continued when a newborn is held safe and secure in her mother's arms.

Your needs are the same needs as your child's, and you do not have to choose between them. That need is connection. Children are a gift. Caring for your child is a sacred trust. The need for parent and child to be close is mutual. Separation from your child is the source of your pain. Disconnection from your child is the price.

Children have to be connected. To be connected, children have to feel good about themselves. Some call this self-esteem or self-worth. Self-worth is the quiet confidence of knowing one's self. To be connected, children have to be loved and feel loveable and learn how to live. They have to be nourished and educated. Both needs are met naturally and easily within a functional family.

Newborns need their mother by their side. Newborns borrow their mother's brain till theirs is ready to take over. Toddlers need their mothers for reassurance as they start to explore and discover the unknown. Teens continue to need their mother's support.

Increasingly, we are forced to deal with the chaos and depravity of feral children. Feral children are the backlash and fallout of a detached society. Feral children do not know love, are unattached, and do not know how to live. Feral children are selfish and self-centered, forever operating in a survival mode based on fear, trusting no one. Feral children lack empathy and the ability to form intimate relationships. A sense of empathy is the hallmark of a humane society. Feral children are disconnected. They are almost inhuman.

Why are we suffering an epidemic of detachment? We are becoming a nation of motherless children. Our society practices the routine separation of newborns and infants, toddlers and teens, from their mothers. This is unnatural, unhealthy, abnormal, and wrong. This is crazy-making. Maternal deprivation is the primary reason for the current crisis, compounded by secondary paternal deprivation or the absence of fathers in the home.

When we add the excesses and abuses of technology and the insanity of consumerism to a parental vacuum, we have created a lethal environment in which to raise our children. Emotional detachment is no mystery in a society which seeks to reduce a baby and his mother to robots — to objects of technology and consumerism. Technology and a preoccupation with the material world leave little time and energy for relationships.

It is vital that parents and society know and understand that *separation of a mother and child is bad* in and of itself. And a secure and enlightened society will not practice the routine separation of mother and child. It is logical that a baby will suffer trauma when separated from his mother, and the stress of separation will alter the biochemistry in his brain. This puts a child into a state of PTSD and reactivity. Mothers and small children have to detach to survive the separation. A pattern of depression and deadness has begun.

Nature designed newborns to be born into their mothers arms and to remain there till ready to leave. When we parent responsively, healthy separation will follow naturally as a child's dependency needs are met. A child will begin to move into independence when compelled to crawl at about nine months, then evolve into mature interdependence.

The biological expectation of newborns is to be close to their mothers. Babies and mothers share a profound bond at birth that, when nurtured as nature mandates, ripens into healthy attachment. An infant's world is empty without her mother. If separated even for a short while, she will suffer a longing for her mother that never dies. Lifelong signs and symptoms such as depression may be unrecognizable as such but are linked, nevertheless, to a lifetime of grieving her loss of self, for mother and child are one at birth.

Insisting that divorce, daycare, TV, a consumer-driven society, parental neglect, and other forms of normative abuse have nothing to do with suffering children is like saying that smoking has nothing to do with cancer, that there was no Holocaust, that the Emperor is clothed in elegant robes. The Emperor is standing in his underwear.

Daycare Is for Adults

I want to be clear about the issue of daycare. Daycare is not for children. Mothers are for children. Mothers are natural, organic. Daycare is artificial and against nature. *And nature always bats last.* There is no substitute for a mother's care. NO ONE can know, care for, or love your child as you, the mother of your child, can. It is every child's birthright to be with his mother. When we separate a child from his mother, we are saying that children have no rights.

We are the parent of our child. But our child is not our parent. A mother's love is unconditional love, but our child's love is conditional! A child will seek our love for many years and will suffer many disappointments. But eventually, after protest and despair, he will give up. Detachment will replace healthy attachment. The natural continuum of connection has been interrupted.

We provide for and protect our child. Though adult children may care for aging parents, our distinct roles with a young child are not interchangeable. Depositing a child in daycare is expecting a child to adapt to the needs of an adult rather than an adult caring for the needs of her child. This is unnatural, unhealthy and wrong.

Daycare is a system of institutional care that cannot give children what they need, no matter how caring or how hard care providers try. Routines and procedures within an institutional setting are based on convenience. How can it be otherwise? For example, the state of Maine's ratio of infants to adult is four to one; toddlers/adult are six to one. Can you see that the things that have to happen one-on-one between mother and child for normal socialization cannot happen when a child is placed in institutional care?

Dropping children off at daycare to be retrieved when convenient is normative abuse. Does this sound harsh to you? Think about how harsh it is for an infant to be separated from her mother. Nature expects infants and toddlers to be in close physical proximity to the one person who loves them. It is in a child's best interests that this person be his natural mother.

Puppies and kittens are not ready to be separated from their mothers before twelve weeks without compromising their socialization. Persons who prematurely separate a kitten from its mother can be reported for abuse. We know that animals who are separated prematurely from their mothers cannot mate, nor can they parent.

It makes sense that the highly sensitive and totally dependent human newborn also needs to be with his mother until ready to leave to learn how to be sociable. *Children are born trusting that their mothers will be with them. The mother-child relationship is founded on trust. Children separated from their mother will never know the best thing in the world: to be with their mother and to be able to depend on her.*

I believe the one-on-one relationship an infant or young child enjoys with his mother predisposes him to repeat an intensely satisfying one-on-one relationship as an adult. I believe multiple care providers during infancy and early childhood predispose a child to repeat that shallow experience with multiple partners as an adult. When our mothers are true to us in infancy, we in turn are likely to be faithful later in life to our partners and to our children.

Daycare mentality is based on survival and leads to a narcissistic society. Narcissism happens when a child's trust has been betrayed and he believes he has to take care of himself because he finds himself to be alone. His mother is not dependable. (The self-centeredness that defines narcissism can also result when a mother is physically present but emotionally unavailable, or cold and withholding.)

The damage to small children attending boarding school commonly is understood and accepted. Incarcerating a child in daycare at six weeks or six months is no different than sending a six-year-old to boarding school. Daycare provides the socialization and stimulation of a prison. Detachment must be the result of a culturally accepted form of parental neglect. This is true for both parent and child. And each generation will visit its agony upon the next.

I gave a workshop on attachment to a daycare blessed with an enlightened director. The providers of this daycare told me that children are better off in daycare because parents do not know how to take care of their children and do not appear to care. The daycare providers told me that children enter daycare on Monday morning, and the only weekend activity they can report is that they watched TV. Parents do not pick up children from daycare even when they can. Teachers in grade school have voiced the same concerns.

It is in the best interests of children and society to ensure that mothers can take care of their babies. We have to nurture mothers so they can nurture their children. Women have to be mothered to mother. There has to be a model of mothering in one's life to learn how to mother. Public policy also must support the critical importance of mothers.

Rabbi Lawrence Keleman has written about the devastation of collective child-rearing in nonparental settings such as the

Kibbutz. This unnatural approach of mass substitutes for day-to-day parental care of children produced sad, dull children incapable of intimacy and masses of mentally ill adults. Families benefit from community support. But it takes a community of *families* to raise children.

Child development expert Edward F. Zigler of Yale University warned that young children placed in daycare centers may be psychologically harmed by the trauma of separation from their mother on a level comparable to the horror of thalidomide. (Thalidomide was a prescribed drug expectant mothers took to alleviate morning sickness. Thalidomide caused severe birth defects.)

I am concerned by a population of women who value working outside the home over being with their infants and small children. I recently overheard a conversation in which a father stated that his wife earned less than the cost of daycare for their two children. This is nuts.

If you are a mother who truly must work to put food into the mouths of your children, then daycare should be your last choice. First, can you work at home? Can each of you work a different shift that enables you to care for your children? If the children are three or older, can Grandma come and care for the children? Grandmas are family and usually love their grandchildren, which makes all the difference. The next choice might be a maternal and long-term nanny and, last, a long-term arrangement in the home of another caring parent. But avoid institutional care.

I have observed a dozen daycares. In all but one of these daycares, the children received attention only during feeding and changing. Those who cried were either ignored or ridiculed rather than comforted. I encountered hostility from the adults present when I attempted to console a little girl who was crying for her mother. Infants in daycare usually give up and typically become apathetic, and toddlers aggressive.

Many daycare providers (and professional social service workers) appear not to know of the actual and developmental needs of infants and children. After a time, many daycare providers become complacent when faced with the impossible task of meeting the many needs of these small children who are so dependent.

Small children who attend daycare are exposed to and suffer communicable diseases many times more than those who do not. Repeated illness is draining to an already immature immune system. Illness is costly to a small child's and family's well-being, and a parent's pocketbook.

Throughout history, due to tragedy such as the death of a mother at birth, some infants have always needed substitute care, but this should be the rare exception.

Knowing what you know now, do you believe daycare could be a form of psychological thalidomide that results in emotionally deformed children?

Daycare is a strange *business*, don't you think? Do you agree that it is time we told the truth about children and daycare?

Please, do everything you can to move heaven and earth to be with your child.

The Disgrace of Drugging Our Children

An elementary school teacher brings a cooler packed with prescription drugs when the class goes on a field trip. Most of the drugs are to control behavior.

Normally, children are naturally active but not frenetic. Why are so many children out of control? Is the way to manage children through the use of drugs? Are children to be controlled? Is the routine practice of prescribing psychotropic drugs good for our children, and if not, then why are we doing it? What should we be doing instead? If all behavior is a response to a need, then to what need are children responding when they are chaotic, disruptive, or defiant? Could children be reflecting the chaos that surrounds them and subsequently internalizing that chaos within? Do you believe that ADD might be DDD (Dad Deficit Disorder)?

Could hyperactivity more accurately be hyper-*reactivity*? Could hyper-reactivity be in reaction to the disruption of the continuum of connection, beginning with the premature separation between a mother and her child? Children who are free-falling in a maternal vacuum are left a legacy of fear and anxiety. What could be sadder than a motherless child? What if a child's mother or father has betrayed her, and either one or both is threatening? Could it be that children need to be outdoors engaging with themselves, others, and the natural world? How often do we see children playing outdoors? Where are they, and what are they doing?

I believe that early childhood trauma can leave a child in a hyper-reactive state of chemical chaos. But the routine prescription of mood-altering drugs as a first recourse is wrong. Drugs are toxic. Drugs have negative side effects. Mixing multiple drugs is potentially dangerous.

Few will deny the value of antiseptics, anesthesia, and antibiotics when used with discretion. Thank goodness for drugs that help children with epilepsy, cystic fibrosis, leukemia. But do we want to model a pill-pushing mentality as a solution to life's problems for our children? Realistic emotions of sadness, grief, frustration, are normal life experiences.

We have to go to the source, to the roots, if we sincerely want to help our children. Much hyper-reactivity is unnecessary and preventable. When we are hyper-reactive, we are disconnected and have become dissociated. To be dissociated means we no longer are in our right mind. We do not think or feel or respond. We react. We can help our children to remain present and in their right mind by doing so ourselves.

Beginning right from the start is the best prevention, and treatment is more of the same. Let us use common sense. Let us start by meeting basic needs: healthful food and drink, adequate rest, appropriate stimulation, plenty of exercise in the sun and fresh air, a stable home with parents who are present, providing a sense of safety and security and belonging, the elimination of toxic stimulation from TV, computers, radios, cell phones, strobe lights, and other forms of disconnecting technology.

It is nuts to suggest psychotropic drugs before suggesting to turn off the TV and to play out of doors. It is easier to prescribe drugs than to prescribe time and attention from parents. Drugs are not a substitute for relationship. Rather, a preoccupation with and dependency upon drugs is counterproductive, getting in the way of the relationship children crave and must have to grow whole.

Please protect your children from drug abuse, both legal and illegal. Selectively, sensitively, limitedly administered, and closely monitored, use of drugs can assist recovery in some cases. But, especially with children, drugs should be given as a last resort and always administered responsibly, deliberately, conservatively, mindfully. Drugs should be used only after all else has been said and done and, even then, in conjunction with commonsense, basic measures.

Much ADHD is preventable by honoring the laws of nature: practicing organic parenting. Ecological parenting means a child who feels secure in her mother's and father's presence, eliminating a toxic environment that includes TV and other technologies, and a strong connection with the natural world from spending much time out of doors. Seldom do children benefit from psychotropic drugs. There is no drug that will treat Parent Deficit Disorder. Children do respond positively when they can feel their parents' presence and loving care.

SUMMARY

The epidemic of detachment is ravaging our children. Many children are not getting their critical needs met for, first, mothering and, then, fathering; neither are they getting the essential needs fulfilled for learning social skills and living skills. Adding insult to injury, we have to add the extreme negative influences of TV and other technologies dictated by consumerism. We are dishonoring the laws of ecology separating children from all that is meaningful, real, and true: their own parents and the natural world. Children feel rejected, lost and confused, alone and disconnected when what they need most and do not receive is to feel connected, *to be close to themselves, with us, and with the natural world.* Operating from a core of fear rather than love, children are telling us of their pain and isolation through their desperate behavior.

It makes sense to prevent disease when we can. We can inoculate our children against most mental/emotional/social and many physical illnesses (the signs and symptoms of detachment) with our caring presence and guidance. We can do this by practicing organic parenting. To raise connected children is our most urgent task.

Children are like flowers.

In the following section we will discuss what we can do to protect our children and prevent the diseases of non-attachment. We will talk about *how to* parent.

The Prevention of Parent Deficit Disorder: Organic Parenting or the Bare Bones of How to Parent

What are ACTUAL needs? The following discussion is loosely based on humanist psychologist Abraham Maslow's Hierarchy of Needs. I have rearranged the order and emphasis.

I believe our first and most important need, our prepotent need, is love. Along with love is the need for affection and belonging. A person may be well fed with nutritious food, but if the need to feel loved and lovable is not met, he will be dead inside. It is a well-known fact that babies in institutions have died for want of love despite force-feeding.

All of us need to feel safe, secure and free. This triad adds up to a *sense of autonomy.* Power and control are nonissues for well-mothered infants and later well-fathered children. But power and control become dominating issues when an infant or small child's need to feel autonomous is treated as nonexistent. When children feel powerless to get their needs met, to feel autonomous becomes more important than anything else. Unmet needs do not go away. They are carried forward into adulthood, manifested in mutated form, to be expressed destructively.

Children must have a strong sense of self-worth. They have to feel good about themselves. Children have a need for appropriate stimulation and a supportive community. Children are born to realize their innate potentials. Nature intends for children to become who they already are. They were born to learn and grow strong and straight and beautiful and give to the world.

Children need appropriate stimulation. Children have physiological needs of fresh air and water, nutritious food and a warm, clean and orderly home.

Once our basic needs for survival are met, our ever-present need to give to others becomes evident. There is nothing better than the feeling we get when helping another. Children love to help. And given the opportunity, children are capable of doing much good in the world.

It is our job as parents to provide our children with what they *actually* need. As a young mother recently told me, "Love and attention are all they really need."

Welcome and Celebrate
Your Baby

*Our days, our deeds, all we achieve or are, lie folded in
our infancy.*

~John T. Trowbridge
The Family Bed by Tine Thevenin

Successful gardeners plan and prepare for their gardens. They learn everything they can before they begin to plant. They take classes at the Cooperative Extension Office. They read gardening magazines and books. They observe other gardens. They talk with folks about gardening and listen a lot. They eagerly listen to the voice of experience of veteran gardeners. They take inventory of their resources such as soil, water, light, time, energy, interest, endurance, physical limitations of self and environment, and finances.

Before you have a baby, plan and prepare for her. "Preparing" does not mean material acquisition, such as a perfect nursery or pram or all that stuff mothers get at baby showers. Babies need very few things. The best gifts friends and family can shower an expectant couple with are a sling, a few thoughtfully selected books, and perhaps a subscription to *Mothering Magazine: The Magazine of Natural Family Living,* and a session with a parent educator/counselor who teaches attachment parenting. A comfortable rocking chair will be a greatly appreciated investment.

Preparing means learning everything you can about what babies need and how you can meet those needs. A list of recommended resources on connected parenting can be found in the back of this book. From the moment you know your child exists, your child is your greatest responsibility. Someone else can do that job at the office or factory. Only you can be the natural mother or natural father to your child.

Are you ready to care for a child? Emotionally, mentally, spiritually, and materially ready? How about your mate? Have a baby only with a spouse who is mature, committed, loyal, responsible, kind and caring; in other words, a person who will be a good father or good mother.

Sometimes, a warm and loving mother can trump a hard father who does not know how to show his love. But a cold and withholding mother and remote/violent father will create a child who has to hide his tender heart inside a hard shell.

If your heart is trapped inside a hard shell, if you had a difficult childhood, you might benefit from meeting with a counselor who is interested, listens, and is kind. Before you have a child, be aware of any harmful baggage you may be carrying. We all inherit our parents' problems. This is not your fault, but it is your responsibility not to harm your children with your problems. Children are *not* resilient; rather, children are malleable, as in maladaptive. You want to leave your child with a healthier and happier legacy.

Children need a safe, warm, and clean home; nutritious food and appropriate clothing; and appropriate stimulation and opportunities for experience. The luckiest children are those who have few store-bought toys and are free to be creative, using their own inner resources, inventing their own toys, making their own fun. Human beings have few needs. What is essential is that your child has you.

The only good reason to have a baby is because you want a baby to love. I believe that babies know when they are wanted and welcomed even before they are born. Unborn babies learn about the world and make connections in the womb. Their mother's familiar voice is a comfort. And if their father is present, his voice becomes reassuring as well. I have read widely and deeply over the last couple decades about attachment. I have been unable to relocate the source yet, but I recall reading a description of research that demonstrated how the beat of a baby's heart will synchronize with a mother's or father's heart. Perhaps this is where we get "two hearts beating as one." *This will not happen with a stranger.*

Consider how you want to give birth: a water birth or not, in a hospital, at a birth clinic, or at home. Where you decide you want to give birth to your baby should depend on where you feel safest and your level of risk. A home birth usually is safest for a low-risk pregnancy. A home birth is usually safest for your newborn, free of drugs, germs, procedures, assuring greater respect regarding your choices for you, baby, family.

You want a safe and peaceful birth for your baby. No matter what your birth experience, trust that you and your baby will find that sense of peace and utter bliss when you hold her close to your heart, secure in your loving arms.

Learn all you can about the effects on your unborn child of taking drugs during pregnancy and childbirth (drug-free is usually safest) and vaccinations for your child (there are life-threatening risks). There are different ways to administer vaccinations to your child if you decide you want your child to be vaccinated. Putting toxins into a tiny body is risky. You can choose to wait until your child is older. I know teens who have never had a vaccination. I know some children who have had just tetanus and polio/whooping cough vaccinations.

Unless there is a true medical reason for circumcision, there is no good reason to circumcise. Your infant boy is born perfect and whole. I cannot imagine the psychological damage resulting from circumcision. And there is risk of the slip of the knife. Should we circumcise little girls? Some folks view circumcision as the sexual abuse of little boys.

A caring and supportive friend of mine reminded me to acknowledge and allow for religious preferences. Years ago, a good friend and I often met with our young sons on the beach during the summer months. Our small boys would play together, and of course, while they played we talked. One day this good mother tearfully told me that she deeply regretted circumcising her son and would not choose circumcision for her son again if she could turn back the clock. The father had been circumcised when he was a baby as was the tradition of their faith and had expected the same treatment for his son.

Because a family member is circumcised is not a reason to continue the practice. Cycles can be broken. Circumcision is a practice that deserves to be challenged. Please do your homework, think clearly, and feel from your heart about your decision. Please be forgiving of yourself if you have practiced the tradition of your faith and find yourself regretful and remorseful. Sometimes, it is easy to know what we should have, could have, and would have done, in hindsight.

Learn about "kangaroo care" or "marsupial care" (wearing your baby close to your heart, a practice increasingly utilized for preemies), which is good for all babies, birth and bonding, baby wearing, the incomparable benefits of breastfeeding, co-sleeping, and the importance of responding promptly to a baby's cry.

Contact your local La Leche League (LLL) and attend meetings. LLL can be one of the best ways to network with other parents who likely believe in and practice attachment parenting.

Different groups have different personalities. If one LLL group does not fit, try another.

Find a homeopathic doctor or a pediatrician and talk to him before you have your baby. You want a physician who will respect you and like your child. Create a support system by surrounding yourself with other folks who are like-minded.

This is the time to clean up your act. I mean this literally. Do you smoke? Drink too much alcohol? Do *any* drugs, either legal or illegal, other than a life-sustaining drug such as insulin for diabetes? Your smoking, drinking irresponsibly, and drugging are bad for your children. Before your child's conception is the time to stop bad health habits. Live a healthy lifestyle. And what is good for your child is good for you. Get help if you need it. Join AA.

If you do not want to stop smoking or using drugs or drinking, stop anyway. Begin "as if" you do feel like it. Work from the outside in so your child can work from the inside out. Rather than yourself, make your child your focus. Everything is easy when you want to do what is best for your child.

Babies need mothers, and mothers need others. The most important other is the father of the child. Babies need families with fathers.

Learn about child development. Learn about how the developing human brain interacts with the environment. The development and life of the unborn child is amazing.

A newborn needs to be held in her mother's arms, to hear her mother's soft, sweet voice, to feel her mother's familiar heartbeat, to look intensely into her mother's eyes, to drink her mother's perfect milk, to be warm and clean. A baby's mother is a newborn's natural environment and appropriate stimulation. As a baby grows, her environment quickly expands to include her father and eventually others.

Do those things with your baby that come naturally: Hold your baby, rock your baby, smile and talk and sing to your baby.

Know that for the first year or more it is normal for mothers to be focused on their babies to the exclusion of almost any other interest. Nature designed mothers that way. The late child therapist, Donald Winnicott, called this "primary maternal preoccupation." As with all things, this will change. And, though there are exceptions, it is usual and normal that babies will prefer their mothers to the exclusion of anyone else. Dads, know that your day will come.

Know that it is okay not to have children. It's okay to have an only child. Be aware that spacing is important. Having children creates more stress on finances, time, and energy. *It is hard to be displaced. If you have more than one child, make doubly sure that the older child feels your love for him.* Siblings usually do better when there are at least several years between them.

Children love to be included and to be helpful. Be sure to thank your children for what they do. But beware of placing too much responsibility on a child's shoulders. I have seen it happen, usually in larger families or single-parent families, that an older sibling (usually sister) is expected to act like second mother. There is a price for precocity — repressed resentment that lasts a long time.

Beware of anyone or anything that would separate a mother and child. This includes pacifiers, cribs, hard plastic seats, playpens, separate rooms, daycare, or other people. The only piece of baby equipment you need is a sling. Babies are wonderfully portable. Babies under a year belong held in-arms. If you do use a stroller as your baby grows older and heavier, rather than use a stroller that faces away from you, use one that faces toward you so your baby can see you and communicate with you. It is best for a baby to remain quietly at home with her mother for the first month of life.

For the human infant, gestation is at least eighteen months: nine months in the womb and nine months in a "womb with a view" in his mother's arms. In the beginning, babies may need their mothers almost 24/7. It is in the arms of his mother that an infant learns *how to* express his love. The primary relationship between mother and child sets the pattern for all other relationships, especially with one's future mate. It is in the arms of his mother where it is first determined whether a child will grow up to be a lover, that a child will learn the dance of connection, that a child will learn to treat those who love him with tender regard. Babies who are refused this nurturing grow up to be fighters and will believe that it is okay to hurt the people who love them. After all, that was done to them. And whatever Mommy and Daddy do is right because Mommy and Daddy are perfect.

Please know, understand, and accept that separation of a mother and her newborn, infant, and small child is harmful. When we separate mother and newborn we create a pattern of detachment that lasts a lifetime and beyond. Separation of a toddler, a six-year-old, or a teen from her mother is bad for everyone. For a child, to be separated from her mother is abandonment. Separation of a mother and child is normative abuse.

Beware of anyone preaching *detachment* parenting to you. Do what *you know in your heart* is best for your baby. Hold and nurse your baby, and let your baby feel the warmth of your unconditional love. Babies and small children are *supposed* to be dependent on their mothers, fathers, and other caring adults. Small children are not meant to self-soothe. Withholding comfort from young children teaches them that the world is a harsh place, indeed. Children who learn that they cannot trust that their parents will meet their natural needs feel betrayed and confused and sad.

Unless babies have a problem such as colic, most babies who are held close to their mothers seldom cry. If your baby does have colic or cries, please always gently hold your baby. Never let your baby cry alone. Would you let an adult cry without attempting to comfort her? You can call LLL for guidance and support if your baby has colic.

A baby's cry is his language. It *should* make you uncomfortable. It should break your heart. A crying baby is telling you something is *seriously wrong*.

Is your child your priority? Children have to be first. Practice heart-service not lip-service. When your child is first, everything else is secondary. When your child is first, then all else is an interference or an annoyance and comes between you and your child. Acceptance of this makes parenting easy. You might resent the housework, phone call, your job or other obligations, but you will never resent your child.

I know an inspiring mother who strives to be honest and fair, and possesses an uncanny ability to get to the heart of a matter. She told me that attachment parenting (AP) was easy to practice with her young son for the first six months and pretty easy through twelve months. After the first year, practicing AP became more of a challenge.

For the first year after birth, mother and babe are the nursing couple, a unit. They pretty much think and feel and do as one. After the first year, a separate self emerges in the developing toddler. This is a necessary step in the move toward independence and eventual interdependence. Some temperaments are more assertive than others. And some mothers have more issues regarding control than others.

Problems need not arise if the focus is not on controlling a child but rather controlling the environment, making it as safe and free for the child as possible, guiding gently by using language of the heart, accepting that being vigilant and available is a given and will soon pass into another stage, keeping in mind that your goal with your child is connection. Ask yourself, "Will my attitude and behavior with my child enhance our relationship or damage it?"

If any behavior, either yours or your child's, is perplexing or frustrating for you as a mother or father, then please find someone to talk to about it. Silent suffering is sad. You may find answers and relief in knowing that your situation is a familiar one with other parents.

Replenish. Restock the cupboard. Take care of yourself. Indulge in a hot shower or bath while Daddy and your munchkin go for a walk. Or a walk in solitude while Dad gives him his nightly bath and reads him a bedtime story. I would get up in the morning before everyone else, make myself something hot to drink, and read for a half hour or so. If a small child woke up, she was usually content to snuggle beside me while I read. After that half hour of restoration, I was ready for a day of caring for others. That little bit of self-care went a long way for me.

A tip about toddlers: Toddlers are learning to master the physical world around them. They are learning to use their muscles and make their arms and legs do what they want them to do. It is usual for a small child to say over and over to his mother and father, "Watch, Mommy!" "Watch, Daddy!" Toddlers want you to recognize and celebrate their growth. Trust your child and be with him on this. Be there and watch how well your child can climb that hill. Smile and say, "Oh, boy! That's so great that you can climb that hill! I'm watching!" Your child wants to share the accomplishments in his life with you.

As in adulthood we are whole only when we have someone with whom to share. Two halves of a whole. A baby does not exist alone. As newborns, our existence is confirmed when we see the affirmation of self reflected in our mother's eyes.

Children who do not receive your affirmation will continue to seek attention throughout their lives, sometimes in destructive ways. And if you want your teen to share her life with you, then you have to begin the pattern of sharing with her when she is small and maintain it.

Be there for your baby, your toddler, your six-year-old, your teen. Make him feel that he belongs. *Include* him in your adult life. It is the exclusion that hurts. Children need to feel that they belong. At about nine months, babies begin the process of healthy separation. They may be compelled to crawl and then walk. You can do your adult work parallel to them as they play by your side. As they grow older, they will both explore farther away from you and want to join you in your work. This is good. This is how children learn to work and how to behave as an adult.

Bedtime

Make going to bed a gentle, mellow time. And make getting up the greeting of a brand-new day!

Nature intends for newborns to remain close to their mothers through the night. Tucking a baby into bed with you is the easiest way to go. Co-sleeping has been practiced in most cultures for most of the history of humankind. Some babies like to lie on top of Daddy, close to his beating heart.

You can place a futon or a folded quilt in your room on a clean floor as your child's first bed for the first couple years. In this way, when you lay your sleeping child down on her nest, she can come to you when she wakes up and climb into bed next to you. Beyond the obvious damage of separation inherent in using a crib, cribs are dangerous. Babies can fall out of cribs when they try to climb out to be with you.

Nursing, rocking, and singing lullabies are sweet ways to end the day together. As your child grows older, you can begin to use a bed in another bedroom and play musical beds. Just relax. Do what works. Be flexible. If you are up at night, catnap during the day. Take it easy. Eliminate nonessentials. Keep life simple. *This time will pass all too quickly.* Soon it will be just a memory.

Everything in its own time. Whether it be planning and serving an elegant dinner party, attending college classes, or taking a vacation alone with your mate, *you will have the time to do everything you want to do.*

Again, *always* lovingly hold a crying baby. Never leave a baby to cry himself to sleep in a separate room, close the door, and close your heart. Your baby will suffer extreme stress and go into shock in a short time. It is distressing to hear any baby cry; it's heartbreaking to hear your own. You will have to detach to let your baby cry. Listen to your heart. Beware of feeling hard and closed. Stay soft and open.

Unless bedtime has become an issue, generally, tired children want to go to bed. They need, want and deserve your reassuring presence as they transition from daytime activity to nighttime sleep. If your child begs for another drink of water it may be because she needs your attention and feels she is not getting it. This applies doubly if your child was separated from you during the daytime.

Connected children do not do things to give you a hard time. A child whose needs are met is a happy child who is able to be a "good" child. All behavior is a response to a need. What is the unmet need behind the behavior?

Have an evening routine: share a bedtime snack, take a bath or shower, brush teeth, read books, turn off the lights and snuggle together while you whisper shared secrets. Stay with her till she is asleep. It's fine if you fall asleep too. Fuss over your child. A bedtime snack of a glass of milk offering calming calcium, or a high protein snack such as cheese and crackers or peanut butter can help her get through the night till breakfast.

Teens also like to be read to. Tucking a teen into bed and sitting in the quiet darkness with her is a time for both of you to talk about things that would often not be uttered in the light of day. Honor their trust in you and listen to their dreams. Savor these moments with your older child. Your child and these shared moments will be gone too soon.

Make getting up a pleasant experience. If your child is an early riser and you are not ready to get up, he can climb in beside you. If he is restless and your house is childproofed, he can look at books or play quietly in his room. Maybe you can have a small snack waiting for him on his child-sized table, such as an apple or a few raisins to nibble on till you get up.

Sleep rhythms are determined by nature. For best results we have to work with nature. Rather than try to control your child's biology, flow with his natural rhythms. A nice tradition to begin when children are young at bedtime is to take inventory of their day: What I have learned today, whom I have helped today, what three things am I grateful for? I am grateful for my phone call with Grandma, the cooing of the mourning doves, Daddy's apple pie for dessert. By your example, teach your child to be joyful, taking a look at the ordinary and seeing it as extra-ordinary.

Make waking up a pleasant experience. It's a new day! Oh, joy! Such possibilities. Begin the morning routine. When we get up, we go to the bathroom, we wash up, brush our teeth, comb our hair, put on clean clothes, put our room in order. We have a nutritious breakfast prepared from real foods at a set table where everyone sits down and eats together. It is best for your child to have no distractions such as phone calls or TV. This is how we begin the day. This is how we live.

Allow enough time to get ready in the morning for anyone who has a time commitment. Hurrying is bad for children. Human beings are not machines made to do things faster and faster or to "multi-task." For best results, let your child do one thing at a time.

Starting the day off on a positive note can make your whole family's day better. If you send your child off to school, make sure her hair is neatly combed, zip up that jacket, be sure she has her hat and mittens on snuggly, and tuck a folded tissue in her pocket. Fuss over her to make her feel special. Remember to hug your child, look into his eyes, and tell him you love him if he goes off to school. And even if he doesn't.

Communication:
Making Contact

Communication is so important in helping our children grow into whole people. But it can be a hazardous journey made more difficult when you don't have a map.

I still am learning how to communicate myself. But I have learned a few lessons that I would like to share with you.

How many wars have been fought, marriages broken, and people made sad and lonely all because they did not know HOW TO express themselves effectively, how to tell others what they feel, and how to request what they need and want? And to do so in such a way that encourages an open heart and mind and continued conversation and mutual understanding?

Again, babies communicate with the language of their cry. We have to respond promptly to a baby's cry. An attuned mother who keeps her baby close to her also has the advantage of reading her baby's body language.

Talk to your baby even before she is born. Describe what is happening to her. In words, reflect her experiences both bad and good. Tell her often and sincerely how much you love her and look forward to her birth. Just as your odor and heartbeat will, your voice will serve as a reference point after your baby's birth.

With a toddler, it works best to go to him if you want his attention. Toddlers need physical contact, such as picking them up or placing a gentle hand on their arm, and then eye contact, depending on the situation. As children grow older, we can use more language and more explanations. We don't pick up our teens, but we can give them a hug. A hug is great body language if a child wants a hug. Always be sensitive to what others are ready for. Respect boundaries. Some of us don't like to be touched when we are upset.

I have discovered that asking works better than telling. Request rather than command, both in conversation and in issuing direction. For example, rather than "This is the best road to take," how about "Do you think this is the best road to take?" "Feed the cat" invites resistance. "Will you please feed the cat, honey?" spoken with eye contact, perhaps a gentle touch on the arm, and a pleasant tone invites cooperation. *It's all about connection.*

Be sure to say what you mean and mean what you say. Match your actions and your words.

WARNINGS!

You want to make contact when communicating with your child. The behaviors detailed in these warnings are counterproductive because they create distance between you and your child. A few of these warnings appear elsewhere in this book because topics overlap.

- Never shout or yell at your child. Loud, harsh voices are scary to a child of any age. It is bad when anyone threatens a child, but it is the ultimate betrayal when parents do. This is because it is our job as mothers and fathers to make our children feel safe.

- Never direct rude, crude, ugly, or violent words (profanity) toward your child. Don't use these words in front of your child.

- Never humiliate your child. His shame will burn in him forever. Humiliation makes a child feel small. And sometimes mean. Humiliation is a precursor to bullying.

- Never ridicule your child. Never call your child names. Never make fun of or use putdowns against your child.

- Never use sarcasm against your child. Sarcasm is humor with ill intention.

- Children love to laugh, and it is good for them to laugh often. But never use humor that hurts your child's feelings. Humor that hurts a person who loves you (or anyone) is not funny. It is disturbing when a behavior does not match a situation; to laugh in reaction to a painful situation feels weird to others.

- Never humiliate a hurting child for crying. Crying is a normal and healthy response to pain and sadness. Connected children do not cry to manipulate.

- Tell your child the truth. If a medical procedure is going to hurt, say so. If you lie to your child they will not trust you. *And without trust you have less than nothing.* Sometimes you will not tell them something because it is inappropriate or could be harmful for them to know. But never lie.

- Avoid using the negating word, "don't." (We will revisit this in "Discipline.") Instead, be positive. For example, rather than yell, "Don't shout!" try, "Please speak softly."

Please speak as respectfully to your child as you would like to be spoken to. Teach your child how to ask for what she needs and wants. The best way is by your example. For instance, if you want something to be done ask your child to do it rather than assume that she knows that you want it to be done and then you are upset because it was not done. Always be fair.

Be aware of your tone of voice. I have heard adults who sound as though they are admonishing their child ahead of time, as though they expect their child to be difficult. It works much better if you use a gentle smile and a friendly, or matter-of-fact tone that implies that cooperation is a given. Children often fulfill your expectations.

If you do not want your two-year-old child to say "no" to you, do not say "no" to her. Say the word "no" rarely, and your child will say "no" only when it is appropriate, such as when asked if she wants a drink, and she does not. Then you can teach a child to say, "No, thank you!"

Hearing the word "no" repeatedly is terribly negating. I know many men and women who reside in correctional facilities. They are wounded children, desperate for love and approval, angry, intensely lonely, grieving. Every person I have met in jail feels unloved and unlovable. To negate means to invalidate, nullify, devalue, render ineffective, *to deny the very existence of.* And there is no mystery to why a person acts as he does when you know his history. I recall a quiet, soft-spoken man who served years in prison for a single tragedy. As a young man, he had plummeted downward on a course of self-destruction, numbed by alcohol that ended with another's death and his own death inside. For him to think of his father is to hear the word, "No."

You can remove the object you don't want your young child to have and put it away where both your child and the object are safe. You are still bigger and stronger than your child; if you don't want him to do something, you can go to him and gently pick him up and remove him from the situation. You can nicely explain that a situation is unsafe without using the word "no." You can be matter-of-fact about it and not make an issue. Or, if the situation is dangerous, you can use a serious voice to convey your concern for your child's safety.

There are at least two parts to verbal communication: speaking and listening. Take your child seriously when she has something to say. Stop what you are doing, face your child, and *listen*. Pay full attention to your child when she has something to say. Practice the skills of a good counselor: Be interested, *listen*, and be kind.

Intrusive questions are a poor way to listen. Instead, if you want more information, reflect on what your child has said to you and let him choose how he will respond. If he has trouble finding the right words to tell you what's on his mind or in his heart, it is all right to help him. State clearly and simply what you think he wants to say. And invite him to correct you if you have misunderstood. I have read that listening is love in action.

Every person has a great need to feel heard, and children are people, too. When a child does not feel heard, he may give up and withdraw, or he may escalate his attempts to gain your attention. One reason children act out is because they do not have the verbal skills to express all their feelings and needs. Children "misbehave" because they feel insecure and frustrated. Again, all behavior is a response to a need.

We have to express who we are. That is why a gardener has to grow, a writer has to author, and a fisherman has to be out on the water casting his net. A mother has to nurture. A child has to be connected to know who he is to express that self. The repression, suppression, and oppression of self-expression can result in aggression toward self or others. Since our true self is love, we aggress when our need for the expression of our love is thwarted. We need to give expression of our true selves and to be heard.

It is good for our children to know how to use "feeling" words. We feel so much more than glad, sad, mad, and bad. Anger is probably the most easily identified emotion by many. But to know only anger is tragically limiting. Helping children to identify and express the nuances of feelings is a wonderful gift we can give children. To know how to express needs and feelings is GOOD for children.

Just to get you started, this is a partial list of words to describe feelings. Notice the different intensities. Add your own feeling words to the list. Get out a thesaurus. There are many words to express the nuances of how we feel! Have fun with exaggerated pantomime and melodramatic play-acting to express feelings. And use them in conversation.

POSITIVE FEELING WORDS

Comfortable, loved, adored, idolized, delighted, friendly, affectionate, alive, vibrant, excited, inspired, amused, relaxed, contented, comfortable, sensitive, sympathetic, concerned, interested, appreciated, peaceful, determined, enthusiastic, capable, worthy, appreciated, optimistic, keen, peaceful.

NEGATIVE FEELING WORDS

Disgusted, frustrated, bewildered, inadequate, embarrassed, guilty, useless, weak, shocked, helpless, regretful, furious, shy, humiliated, alienated, horrified, disturbed, rejected, timid, confused, sullen, alarmed, annoyed, outraged, contemptuous, disdainful, alarmed, troubled.

One way we teach children vocabulary is to *read* to them. Another way we can teach children how to speak is by talking with them. It is a hoot to talk with infants. They are so adorable when they answer you. Try it. You will fall in love with them.

Never say, "Hurry up!" to a child (or anyone). Give your child the time he needs to get to where you want to go. Go to your child and cheerfully help your child to get ready and out the door.

Never count at your child, "One, two, three . . . ." Would you like someone to count at you?

A word about shopping with children. Shop with children only when you need something. And first make sure your children's basic needs have been met: It helps when children have been fed, are rested, have used the bathroom before leaving the house. It is natural for children to want to touch in a store. They see you touching. And for children, often, to see is to touch. Connected children touch appropriately and are seldom a problem. Connected children will stand quietly by a parent while their parent looks at things or talks. These children seldom ask for anything. Shopping with them is easy.

Children who run rampant and leave a wake of disorder scattered behind them or plead incessantly for everything are not ready to be in a store. It is disconcerting to hear a parent yelling at a child not to touch or "Come here" while the child is paying no attention.

If a connected child *really* wants something, even if you cannot buy the object be sympathetic. "You really want that teddy bear, don't you! I am so sorry I can't buy it for you right now."

Distraction can be a useful strategy for very young children when they want what they cannot have. You can often trade an object by offering another to them.

Most "temper tantrums" can be prevented if you consider the needs of your child. A connected child does not manipulate. He is expressing how he feels, and he needs to know that his feelings are important to you. If your connected child has a "temper tantrum," he needs you. He needs to feel your concern and not the betrayal of your anger. What other people think is unimportant.

A meltdown means your child has reached her limit. You can calmly pick her up and carry her out of the store. Or you can quietly sit by her and wait till she is through, reassuring her that you understand her frustration and that you love her. The worst thing you can do is to desert her emotionally or physically. A temper tantrum is body language that tells you that she is having a hard time and feels disconnected. Perhaps more was expected of her than she was reasonably and realistically able to handle; something was done to her, said to her, or has happened to her. We are the adults, and our child is depending on us to help her return to harmony and balance.

Two communication tips: With an older child, forget the mechanical dishwasher. Good conversation often occurs while in the kitchen cleaning up after dinner. With one washing and one drying, the setup is perfect. Girls tend to like direct eye contact. But some boys prefer the parallel talk that happens while working alongside each other. Invite your son to help you with kitchen duty and talk.

Another opportune time to talk is driving along in the car. Turn off that radio and listen to each other. Riding in companionable silence is nice. Stop the noise so you can hear yourself think and so you can feel.

You will give your child a gift if you can model healthy discussion, even passionate disagreement. Healthy disagreement is honest, objective, constructive; it's never cruel or vicious. It feels great to agree, but we can also disagree graciously when we listen openly and with interest and care about the other person and her point of view. We can learn from a differing point of view. Connection does not have to mean having the same outlook or beliefs; it can mean meeting another person at the point where he is and appreciating each other's differences.

We can teach our children by our responses that nonviolent communication is the way to build a bridge of mutual respect and understanding between differences. When another person feels unheard or threatened and attacks us verbally, we can choose not to return in kind. We can refrain from name-calling and profane speech. We can use "I" statements: I feel, I want, I need.

We can remember that deep sadness usually precedes anger. Anger is often a secondary emotion. Listening with our heart, we can focus on and identify with underlying needs such as the need for respect, understanding, acceptance, belonging and respond gently. If necessary, we can simply walk away. Protective violence is a last resort.

Once, in amazement, I witnessed a five-year-old girl calmly negotiate a problem between two other five-year-old girls in a sandbox. The negotiator stood between the girls who were fighting, turned to one to learn what she had to say and then to the other. She then offered a solution to each and asked if her suggestions sounded reasonable to both. You had to see it to believe it. And peace returned to the sandbox. This skilled young diplomat had learned how to consider and accommodate the needs of others from her exceptional parents.

Model quiet sincerity and unfailing courtesy when dealing with tradesmen, a service provider, or the public if there is a problem to be dealt with. Teaching your child how to focus on the solution rather than the problem in a nonconfrontational manner is a valuable gift.

Be sure to tell your child you love him. Children of every age love to hear their mothers and fathers say to them, "I love you!" Watch your child glow! "I am so glad you are mine!" "I am so glad you exist!" As adults they will repeat those words to their partners and children. Children love to hear their parents say, "I love you!" to each other.

Remember that children need the communication of touch. A hug, a pat on the shoulder, a kiss on the cheek, holding them on your lap while you talk with them or read to them, or snuggling together at bedtime tells them that you love them, as do words.

Visualize the tall adult way up there and the short child way down there. Close the physical distance between you and your child. Squat down or pick her up. Hold her on your lap. Level your eye contact when speaking to a child. Children do not respond well to distance. Children need to hear words. We humans are speaking creatures. But children also need appropriate touch. Infants deprived of touch die. Older children shrivel up inside and want to die.

If your child does not hear "I love you!" from you when he is young, he might not know how to say those three words later. Love is our greatest hunger, even before food or drink. Never assume that your child knows you love him. *Silent love is heard as indifference,* as though your child is invisible to you! Nothing could be more painful. Nothing. Tell your child, "I LOVE YOU!" often and with all your heart.

# Discipline Means to Teach

Punishment and discipline are often confused. Indeed, the more punished the less disciplined.

We welcome folks who practice good manners, are considerate of others, and behave appropriately. Connected parenting is not permissive. Connected parenting believes in gentle guidance. Connected parenting is not based on fear. Connected parenting is based on trust, is based on relationship.

Discipline means to teach. Discipline is positive and helpful; it tells and shows a child *how* to behave. And knowing *how to* behave feels normal, feels great. Discipline is encouraging. Discipline is a gentle smile, a warm hug. Discipline makes order out of chaos, explains away confusion, shows us the way, helps us feel sane, assures us we are not alone and that we can trust those who care for us, and makes us feel connected.

Discipline and punishment are opposites.

Punishment is negative and hurtful. It fails to teach a child how to behave, which defeats our purpose, and makes a child feel bad. Punishment is discouraging. Punishment wears a menacing face. Punishment is cold withdrawal or frightful attack. It creates chaos and leaves us feeling bruised and confused and crazy, blamed and shamed, isolated, betrayed, and disconnected.

Punishment does not work. It is power *over* when what we want is power *within*. Punishment creates negative energy, which attracts more negativity. People behave badly because they do not feel good about themselves. How a child feels about herself is the key to how she behaves. How anyone feels about herself is critical to every aspect of her life. When we feel good about ourselves we radiate positive energy attracting and creating more good positive vibrations. We are connected to our true self. We know who we are.

Sticks and carrots are equally bad for children. Both punishment and rewards are manipulative and insulting. Gold stars, grades, time-out, withholding food or privileges are bad for children. If a child goes out in the rain, a child will get wet. That is a natural consequence. If a small child pounds the living-room table with a hammer rather than the two-by-four provided and does not stop pounding on the table when asked to hammer the board of wood, the hammer gets put away for a while till we are ready to try again. That is a logical consequence. But denying a child ice cream because of the hammer incident is unproductive because the two instances are unrelated. Food or any unrelated loss of pleasure is counterproductive to our purpose, which is to help a child learn how to live. We do the right thing the right way because that is how we live. Punishments and rewards are irrelevant.

A caution about time-out: Time-out segregates and further disconnects an already disconnected child. Children usually are difficult because they feel distance between themselves and their parents — because of insecurities or because they are not getting some important need met, such as attention. If a child is upset and needs time to calm down and you believe removal of your child from a situation will help, that is fine, but do not remove her from your reassuring presence. *Be with her* and avoid pushing her into further isolation. Take a walk together. Use the calming and harmonizing influence of Mother Nature to help discipline your children.

Hugs are a great way to discipline your child. You can teach your child to come to you and ask you for a hug when she is feeling upset. Make a couple of mugs of hot chocolate and sip them together in the kitchen or wherever you can be alone together. Create an atmosphere in which reconnection can happen. You do not want to control or manage your child's behavior. You want to go to the source of your child's pain, which underlies misbehavior. You want your child to know she is loved. A child who feels loved does not misbehave. You don't even have to mention the misdeed. A child knows when what he has done was unacceptable. Children who behave unacceptably do not feel good about themselves. You want to restore that connection within themselves. This is because they will naturally behave when they feel good. Just be with your child. Hold her on your lap, hold her hand, and listen when she is ready to speak.

Manipulative praise is bad for children. The intent of manipulative praise is to control a child's behavior. An authentic expression of appreciation is good for your child. Spontaneous praise is wonderful! Spontaneous praise affirms and is encouraging. Spontaneous praise comes from the heart. "Oh! What a beautiful picture! I love the colors." "These chocolate chip cookies taste so yummy! Daddy will love them."

Also, never pretend your child has a choice when he does not. There are at least two occasions when this can happen. One is when a reward such as a gold star is offered for the completion of a behavior. The adult informs the child that when the child is "good" and does what the adult wants him to do, he will get a gold star. The adult calls this an "agreement." When the child does not follow through, he has broken the "agreement." But what part did the child have in making the "agreement"? And then he is shamed by not receiving the gold star. Sometimes, a child becomes so shamed that he no longer cares; he is beyond feeling shame or anything else about the situation.

The other occasion is when no choice is intended and a child is offered a choice. "Would you like to go home now?" "No" is one appropriate answer. And you will confuse your child when you do not honor her "no." Instead say, "It's time to go home now, Honey." And expect cooperation. If your child has a hard time transitioning, give her a heads-up by telling her five minutes ahead of time that you will be going home in five minutes. Help your child pick up the toys and put them away; help her put on her coat and say good-bye. Be calm and understanding, knowing that it can be hard to leave friends when you are having a good time together.

Children do not always know what is appropriate behavior for a particular situation. It's up to us to teach them by both example and preparation. For example, how do we behave in most museums? Before you go to the museum, you can explain to your child about appropriate museum behavior: We speak softly; we walk; we stay close to the adult who brought us; we do not touch with our hands, we look with our eyes. And we can add why this is important. If necessary we can put our hands in our pockets or behind our backs, which I have done as a model for children while visiting a museum.

Depending on whom you are visiting, if there are no other children to go outside to play with, you can teach your child that when we visit another person's home we can listen quietly while adults talk (the same when visiting a doctor's office). Many connected children do this naturally without deliberate instruction. (Nothing was so interesting to me as a child as being allowed to stay and listen to adult conversation. This is a way we learn about the mysterious adult world).

We ask permission *before* we reach out and touch, open a door, and so on. And we respect the answer. We are on their turf. We have to be considerate of others when in a public setting. If a child cannot sit quietly to enjoy a movie, that child may not be ready to attend a theater. The same for dining out in restaurants other than fast-food restaurants. It is disruptive and unfair to others when a child is noisy or restless. And it is unfair to a child to have to sit still when he is not ready. Babies in-arms are easy because they are content to be held.

Teaching a child what is appropriate behavior for a particular social setting encourages confidence and competence. Knowing how to behave protects a child from disapproval for doing what he should not do and not doing what he should. How can children learn such things if we fail to model such behavior and coach them?

Children need discipline in the true sense of the word. The strongest discipline for a child is the love you both share. This is the *affection connection*. This is where your greatest influence lies. Connected children are *easy*. They want to cooperate and please you. They are a joy!

WARNINGS!

- Never strike your child. Even once, and you may destroy the trust your child has in you. And in himself. It is confusing when someone you love hurts you. It does not make sense.

- Never humiliate your child. A child will remember that humiliation forever.

- Never call your child names for the sake of "discipline" or for any other reason.

- Never use profanity against your child or even in your child's presence. Ugly language is disrespectful. Ugly language is intended to insult. Ugly language is violent. Your child is a gift. Treat your child with REVERENCE.

- In general, teasing is a bad idea. Either avoid or be very cautious about teasing. Playful teasing has to be done within the context of a secure relationship. Teasing has to be gentle and mutually enjoyed. Teasing that hurts another is never okay.

- Never tickle your child. Tickling is invasive and disturbing. Tickling is usurping your child's right to have power over his body. TICKLING IS BAD FOR YOUR CHILD. Tickling is normative abuse.

- Never encourage your child to be a wise guy by egging him on. Wise guys are unreal. To be a wise guy is to create emotional distance between self and others for protection. To be a wise guy is to wear a mask to hide the fear of appearing vulnerable. Be unafraid. Be authentic.

- Never scream or yell at your child. This is frightening to a child. FEAR IS BAD FOR YOUR CHILD!

- Never deliberately try to scare your child. This teaches a child to be fearful. Parents represent safety. To be the source of fear is betrayal.

- The best rules are positive rather than negative; they remove obstacles rather than implant them, help rather hinder, and facilitate. Commonsense rules are necessary to keep us safe.

- You are the parent. Never argue with your child. You are kind and respectful. You can explain an issue age-appropriately, and you can discuss. You are not mean or heavy or threatening. Your child depends on you to be the adult and to protect him and keep him safe, to make wise decisions, and to follow through. Your expectation is that your child will cooperate. If expectations are reasonable, confrontations rarely happen with connected children. Give your child as much freedom as is safe. Say "yes" often and "no" rarely. If an ordinarily cooperative child resists, then perhaps he is not ready and you should listen and reconsider your request. This is responsive parenting.

A connected child is easy to discipline and to be with. A disconnected child can be hard. Connected children know. A word or a look is often all that is needed to guide them. Always speak kindly to your children. Remember the Golden Rule: *Treat others as you would like to be treated.* CHILDREN BEHAVE AS THEY ARE TREATED.

Discipline for infants under one year consists of your loving care. For the terrific twos, you have to be with them. RIGHT there with them. Most healthy toddlers are active and curious but not wired. They love to sit on your lap and listen to a story. Sometimes many stories. You have to be attuned to them. You have to keep a listening ear, a watchful eye, and an open heart about you. *Control the environment* (rather than the child). Make her surroundings friendly and self-limiting. A safe environment is good discipline. Again, let your child be as free to explore and investigate as is safe. Outdoor play is great.

A well-kept secret is the use of hugs to help discipline a child. HUGS ARE GOOD FOR CHILDREN. Instead of scolding a child, sit down in the rocking chair and take her into your lap. Or, with an older child, give her a hug and reconnect. One of the hallmarks of a functional family is that they disconnect from each other less often, less severely, and they know *how to* reconnect. Often, a connected child will respond readily to a hug.

> *We need 4 hugs a day for SURVIVAL. We need 8 hugs a*
> *day for MAINTENANCE.*
> *We need 12 hugs a day for GROWTH.*
> ~ Virginia Satir

I would like to address one situation I see repeatedly with younger children. A parent stands across a room or parking lot and yells at the child to do something; not to do something; or to come. "NO, Jane! NO!" The child does not respond. It does not work to yell at children across a room. YOU HAVE NO CONNECTION. Either the parent gets ugly or gives up. GO TO THE CHILD. If he is little, just go to him, softly tell him what you are doing, and gently scoop him up.

If a child is older, go to her, squat down to her eye level. You can draw a small child close to you or touch an older child on the shoulder — after speaking to her and facing her first. Tell your child what you need and want from her. You can go to a child and take her little hand and lead her.

Teens need their parents in their lives, and what you do will be noticed and have influence with your teen. But your child is done in the discipline department by the time he reaches the teen years. Either he is secure, or he is struggling. The ball is in his court. I am NOT saying hands off. I am saying that either a pattern of connection has been established, or it hasn't by now. Your teen will now reflect you. Children are a mirror to their parents. Disconnected teens who do not identify with their parents may seek belonging elsewhere. This is where other caring adults can step in and help your teen where you might not be able to.

When you give your child a direction, frame it in the language of encouragement. Be stingy when using the word "don't."

Use it when you want to cease a behavior now. Otherwise, positively state what you want. When you want your child to do something, just ask him to do it. The common method is to say, "Don't forget!" But the word "don't" can make us feel chastised, as though we did something bad already! It feels negating. Instead, say, "Please remember!" It feels great! The internal response to that request feels like, "Oh, thank you!"

Again, watch your tone. Listen to yourself as you speak to your child. Do you sound like you are expecting your child to misbehave? Smile when you speak, putting a smile in your voice. Expect your child to want to behave.

Spilled milk happens in life. We learn the skill of pouring by spilling. Some of us spill more than others. And we can set a child up to succeed by pouring water in a plastic cup in the tub or sink or outside where it does not matter. If we do spill milk we wipe it up and try again. It's not a big deal.

When giving a small child liquid in a cup, pour an inch or so at a time. Then there is little to spill. When you know what your child can and cannot do, you might anticipate a "spill" if you can, and circumvent it with your own cleverness! Prevention is always worth more than cure.

Note: Mistakes that involve the safety of anyone or intend ill will toward another call for intervention. When a child intentionally tries to hurt another person the message is clear that something is wrong. Both victim and perpetrator need to feel your love. We teach our children how to deal with attacks from others by standing up for them when they are defenseless. When they are ready, they will know how to do this for themselves. And they will know to protect others.

It is our job as parents to keep our children safe. I have seen young, securely attached children, walking on the road with their parents, warn them a car is coming and, on their own, go to the side of the road. You cannot sit in your lounge chair, talking on your cell phone, and expect your child to listen to you yelling across the yard to stay out of the street. For many children, you have to pay attention and BE THERE WITH YOUR CHILD, right by her side.

Many securely attached young children will be happy to play with you in sight and sound of them as you do your adult work. They may work with you and perform adult tasks remarkably well. Many children are capable and competent if we spend time with them and allow them to try without instilling fear in them.

"Misbehavior" is usually due to insecurities and is the expression of that pain. Often, what we read as "misbehavior" may be due to a child's understandable lack of knowledge about a matter, natural curiosity, lack of size and physical strength, or lack of skill. These are nothing to get angry about and will "correct" themselves in time as children grow more worldly with our modeling, guidance, understanding, and acceptance. Minor trespasses can be overlooked.

"Consistency" is another word one often hears in reference to raising children. I think the consistency children need is in our unconditional love and responsiveness to their needs. We have to be flexible when it comes to situations. What is appropriate at home may not be appropriate in public. What is appropriate while playing outdoors is not suitable while indoors. And what is appropriate at one time may not be at another time. Your child might play pirates on the stairs, shouting "Ahoy, Matey!" every afternoon for a week, having a grand time. But he is careful about playing quietly when Great-grandma comes to visit Sunday afternoon and needs to rest in the guestroom.

We respond to each child as an individual with different levels of need and temperament. All children have to eat, but their tastes and appetites are unique and will change with age and stage. We have to be consistently *responsive* to each developing child. We have to be consistently kind.

For the first year, babies want to be held in their mother's arms. They are like little Velcro babies. As newborns, babies often want to nurse a great deal. This is normal and desirable. Children in-arms are often in the quiet-alert stage. Slings can be a great aid at this time. You do your adult activities as you can. Children are spectators. And they are learning. You do hug and kiss them, rock and sing to them. You are an adult who has work to do and interests to pursue and you do them. You remain with your child and do your work. Right now, being productive often means giving your baby the time she needs.

After the first year of wearing your baby, children begin to play parallel to you or you can include them. They will want to imitate you. This is good. They will learn from you, watching your confident competence.

Children have to observe and *to learn* social skills and the skills of daily living. And they learn most by observing our adult behavior. It is unrealistic and unfair to expect children to behave as miniature adults. Again, children need you by their side to borrow your intelligence until they have developed their own. This is how they learn.

Children are just like flowers. *When their needs are met, they blossom. They are happy, and a happy child is able to be a "good" child.*

Fathering

> *I cannot think of any **need** in childhood as strong as the*
> ***need** for a **father's protection**.*
>
> ~Sigmund Freud

ood, strong men provide for and protect children. It is *good* for children when their father's commitment and loyalty are toward his own family. Mothers depend on the father of their child for both material and moral support. Fathers make it possible for a mother to be what she should be: a mother nurturing their children. Though infants naturally reach first to their mothers for comfort and security, by the age of two or so, children crave a daddy. They may become tearful when he leaves them.

Boys without fathers are at risk of becoming rogue elephants. When a herd of elephants in Africa was without mature males, adolescent elephants were killing rhinoceros because they could. When adult males were imported, the killing stopped. Boys learn from their fathers how to behave as men.

Girls learn from fathers what to expect from men. How does daddy treat mommy and me? Does he make me feel safe? Is he there at all? Girls who do not have strong and protective fathers who are there for them and care about them are at risk of looking for love and affection in dangerous places and for making bad choices in choosing a partner.

It is important that fathers teach their sons by their own manner and behavior to respect women and to teach their daughters that they deserve respect. The reverse is true as well. We want our sons to grow up to be honorable, to be gentlemen, and our daughters to grow up to be gentlewomen.

The complementary role of fathering to mothering is necessary for the completion of raising a whole child. Can you imagine the Earth without the Sky? Father Sky is the Teacher to Mother Earth the Nurturer. This is the way of things.

Developed and caring fathers are *good* for children.

Fathers are necessary.

Grandparents

Kind and accepting grandparents are *good* for children. Grandparents can be the saving grace in a family. They can ease trouble between children and the world (including parents). They can enrich a child's life with their experience and history. They can provide depth and orientation. Knowing our roots helps to ground us. Our past is part of our future.

Grandparents have stories to tell about when our parents were little and about family characters. And children love to hear these stories and treasure them all their lives. Grandparents *love* their children. When grandparents and grandchildren know each other, grandparents are the obvious stand-ins for parents.

It is worth considering living nearby grandparents. If there is geographic distance between grandparents and grandchildren, it is good for grandparents to make an effort to make contact often, such as writing frequent letters. Children can write grandparents back, cultivating the lost art of letter writing. Send a recording in your voice of a book on tape; or narrate and record family stories as a personal treasure only you can give to your grandchildren.

Children benefit when they have caring grandparents in their lives. Three cooperative generations living under the same roof make good economic sense, and more helping hands can alleviate the stress of one or two adults having to do too much alone.

Warning! Beware of grandparents (or anyone) who are of the old school. These are grandparents who believe children should fear adults. They are people who believe that to pick up a crying baby is to spoil it, that a crying baby "just" wants attention, that corporal punishment such as spanking is appropriate, that children should be seen and not heard. They adhere to rigid toilet training, forcing a child to eat what he does not like, and so on. These people are to be avoided.

Show your children how we take care of our elderly parents, our children's grandparents. Your now elderly parents took care of you when you were little, young, and dependent. Now it is your turn to take care of the two people who gave you their time, energy, money, and unconditional love. Show your children how we take care of those who have loved and cared for us. If you do not care for your aging parents, you will wish you had. Too often, we do not know what we had till it is gone.

Learning Is to Bring Forth

hildren are born learning. Birds fly, fish swim, and humans learn. It comes naturally. If a child is nourished, he will feel safe, be free of fear, and be able to attend. The Waldorf schools have a nice approach to education, which is *"to bring forth."* It is all already there. A child can become what he already is. Within every seed is a flower waiting to unfold. When we honor our child's highest inner self, the gift that all children bring to this life will develop.

One of our roles as parents is to be good models and mentors for our children. We are their first and most influential teachers. This gives us amazing power to shape our children's lives. Intellectual development is interactive with the environment. Every organism has an optimal environment. For newborns that environment is primarily their mother. When an infant feels safe and secure in his mother's arms, he often is in the quiet-alert stage. He absorbs everything around him. If what he witnesses is good and sane, he can make sense of it.

Toddlers are curious little folks. Their world is ever expanding. But they want their mothers available even when they are checking out what's in the next room. Three-year-olds will go with Daddy to the hardware store and wave good bye to Mommy. Five-year-olds will visit a neighbor. Children traditionally attend kindergarten at five or six years of age because most children are beginning to separate naturally from their mothers and families at that age.

Children are not ready to be separated routinely from their mothers before the age of at least six years, and possibly older. When we interrupt nature's plan of gradual separation, we instill fear in a child. And fear interferes with learning. Boys often need to wait till eight years of age before they are ready for routine separation from their mothers and families. If a child protests separation, he is telling you that he is not ready.

When our children are connected they know who they are and what their interests are. We can take pleasure in helping our children pursue their interests, *to bring forth* — and step out of the way if that is appropriate. Being connected — knowing who we are — is also important for adults in choosing a profession that fits and is right for us.

Most children attend public school. If your child attends institutional education, advocate for your child to have a teacher who loves children, learning, and life. Be visible and involved. Get to know your child's teacher, the principal, and the other students. School districts and individual schools have differing philosophies to teaching and learning. Teaching based on building on students' strengths and managing weaknesses seems best. Protect your child against unreasonable busing.

In many communities, with the interest and support of their families, children actively participate in organized (and usually competitive) sports. These families often are interested and involved, with parents faithfully attending games. Sports for many of these children is all about belonging — being part of a team. But I have heard of schools spending twenty thousand dollars on football but having no money to purchase library books or graph paper. If your child's school is crying poverty, suggest that the desirability of competitive sports that involve costly uniforms, equipment, and busing be reviewed. Children need fresh air, sunshine, physical activity, fun, opportunities to learn how to work cooperatively with others and to learn good sportsmanship. Grabbing a bat, a ball, and a few baseball gloves and having an informal game during recess or after school is the way to go. And it costs little.

As in homes, schools have to make children feel safe. To feel safe is a high need for children. Fear is *bad* for children. They cannot attend to matters at hand if they feel afraid. Children have to feel free of fear to be able to learn. Children of *all ages* who attend school need to come home to a parent who is waiting for them with a hug.

Children who are emotionally impoverished have the same difficulty attending to lessons as do children who have not eaten a nourishing breakfast. Many children are hungry for both love and food. First things first. Children have to be well nourished (love and food) if they are to be well educated.

Once, public education believed every child deserved a community school. Children did better in the small one-room school houses to which they could walk and often go home for lunch. Some smaller rural community schools in which caring teachers and administration preside can still offer your child the quality of relationship that is conducive to learning.

If you are concerned about sending your young child to public school because of the chaos often dominating classrooms; the depersonalization of consolidation, bullying, negative socialization, squashing your child's love of learning, long bus rides with children who shout obscenities or perform undesirable services, the terrorization and violation of children by public school sex education — to name just a few deeply concern-provoking issues — then you might want to consider homeschooling. There is a strong network of homeschooling parents who can provide you with support and share teaching abilities. One mother who knows fluent Spanish can exchange giving lessons with another family whose father is fluent in French.

Older homeschoolers often become un-schoolers. By age twelve or so, children who are homeschooled engage in self-study. They no longer require much direction.

The experiences of homeschooled children have the potential for richness and diversity and positive socialization. Homeschooled children enjoy hands-on learning. They can spend time with adults, observing adult behavior. They interact with the entire age spectrum. The behavior and intellectual capabilities of homeschooled children can be superior. These children are able to listen and to cooperate.

Our best learning happens within the context of a caring relationship. Homeschooled children have ample one-on-one opportunities to learn. In general, I have found homeschooled children to be intelligent, imaginative, creative, enthusiastic, eager to learn, curious, cooperative, courteous, respectful, responsible, caring, competent, confident, helpful, and mature. They are able to make informed and mature decisions. Children who attend public school who possess these qualities usually have very interested and involved parents. In essence, these children who attend public school are also homeschooled.

There are some good, small private schools. Be sure to keep your finger on the pulse of any school your child attends. If you feel anxious about sending your child to a school, then find an alternative that will be healthy for him. You have done such a good job to raise a child who trusts, and loves to learn. Why sacrifice your precious little boy or girl to a system so it can perpetuate itself? Homeschooling is a natural continuation of organic parenting.

Not all of us are interested or have the aptitude to go to college. There is much meaningful work in the world that needs to be done that does not require a college education. Some younger folks are not ready to go to college but might be when they are older after they have had more experiences.

Apprenticeship programs seem to be a natural way to learn a trade or craft. A learning experience that allows a person to learn comprehensively and thoroughly a trade from bottom-up, hands-on, alongside a master makes sense.

Many self-actualized adults were homeschooled and enjoyed a close relationship with their mothers. You may know some of them. Abraham Lincoln, Thomas Edison, Robert Louis Stevenson, and Rachel Carson are among them.

Your child will learn eagerly and effortlessly if she feels free and safe, if you create an atmosphere of exploration and discovery with the raw materials, interesting people, and exposure to ideas and opportunities for hands-on experiences, and if she is allowed to follow her own interests. And she will meet any presenting challenges with confidence and maturity.

Manners Matter

*Consideration for others is the basis of a good life,
a good society.*

~Confucius

All people have to be considerate of others. As sentient beings, we all have to be sensitive to how our behavior influences others. Children are innately kind. Unless mistreated, children want to be sociable; but the skills of *how to* are learned. Little children especially will learn by observing you.

Children can learn how to:

- Greet people in person — smile, extend your hand, look that person in the eye, speak your name.

- Use telephone manners: both in placing a call — "Good Morning, Mrs. Smith. This is Sally. May I please speak with Jane?" "Thank you!" — and in answering the phone.

- Say "please," "thank you," and "you're welcome." Say "thank you" often.

- Acknowledge a gift with a handwritten thank-you note and/or a phone call. A thank-you note received in the mail is nicer than an e-mail.

- Say "Excuse me" when passing in front of another, burping, or leaving the dinner table.

- Cover their mouth and nose with their arm if they sneeze or yawn. And use a handkerchief or tissue to blow their nose.

- Use a fork, spoon, knife, and napkin correctly.

- Wait their turn respectfully. Waiting is a part of life and not something to make others feel bad about.

- Wait politely while others are engaged in conversation and interrupt only if there is an emergency.

- Be on time for appointments.

- Dispose of trash properly. Littering is an abomination.

- Take their hat off when entering a building or sitting down at a table to eat.

- Keep shoes off furniture.

- Check to see if anyone is behind them when they pass through a door and then hold the door open for that person. Hold the door open for a mother with a baby, any elderly person, any person carrying a large or heavy package.

- Be polite to anyone who is providing a service.

- Use crosswalks when crossing a street and stop to look both ways before crossing. Wave a thank-you when a driver stops.

- Walk on the sidewalk if there is one. Acknowledge others — move aside to let oncoming folks pass. If there is no sidewalk, walk opposite oncoming cars. Walk in single file on a busy road, which is safer for everyone.

- Sincerely offer the other person the last piece of pie. Or share it.

- Clean up their mess; if we use a plate we wash it. We leave the kitchen as clean as or cleaner than we found it.

This is how we live. This is how we behave. This is how we are everyday, all of the time. We treat each other respectfully and kindly. Teach your child to take accountability for his behavior and apologize when he makes a mistake or hurts another's heart. Teach your child to respect the privacy and property of others. This includes:

- Knocking on a closed door and waiting for an invitation before entering.

- Not opening and reading another's mail, not listening to another's phone calls, and so on.

- Asking and waiting for an answer before assuming that we may use the property or belongings of others. This includes that of siblings. And to respect the answer should it be no.

Teach your child to be sensitive to personal space. Personal space is a circle that surrounds every one of us and travels with us. For some people it is more than for others. We do not enter into another's personal space without permission. Reaching into someone's personal space to touch an earring, for example, can be very unsettling for that person. Obvious exceptions are mothers and infants, or spouses and significant others — because they are one. Their personal space is much the same space.

Asking questions for information about a subject is usually encouraged. But asking personal questions of strangers can be intrusive. Teach your child to be sensitive to and respectful of emotional and intellectual boundaries.

Always be willing to stop and help anyone in need. *Always* be kind.

You probably can think of other ways we can treat others with consideration. Manners are the grease for the wheels of a civilized society.

This is how we live.

Modeling and Heroes

Do your work the best you can,
and be kind.
~Natalie Goldberg,
Writing Down the Bones

We have to model the behavior we want to see in our children. What do we want them to learn? They will learn what we do.

One summer evening as I tended my vegetable garden, a dad who lives in the neighborhood dropped by for a chat. He told me that he had been outside with his soon-to-be-two-year-old son. The dad had been leaning against the house with one foot crossed over the other, smoking, the cigarette cupped in his hand. Looking down, he had seen his son beside him, leaning against the house, one foot crossed over the other, holding an imaginary cigarette to his lips, cupping it in his little hand in exact imitation of his hero father. The dad told me that he knew he had to stop smoking, and soon.

You can teach positive habits to your child as illustrated by this example of modeling: A few years ago I attended a discussion group of about twenty women of all ages, including a young mom and her little girl who also was soon to be two years old. The discussion lasted for about an hour and a half. During that time, the little girl quietly sat on her mom's lap, with an occasional word spoken softly between them, and sipped orange juice from a fast-food cup that has a lid with a straw stuck through the middle. When the juice was gone, the mom placed the cup on the floor beside the chair. At the end of the discussion, as everyone rose from her chair and without prompting, the little girl picked up the cup, walked over to the garbage can standing in a corner about ten feet away, dropped the cup into the can, and returned to her mom.

The little boy naturally imitated his father's smoking, and likely, so did the little girl copy her mom's taking responsibility in tidying up after herself. Neither was *told* to do what they did. They learned from what they saw their parents do.

We all know to err is human. It's part of the process of becoming. We try to learn from our mistakes so we don't repeat them, take responsibility for them, clean up our mess, apologize and continue on. We would not be human if we never made a mistake. Do any of us want to be inhuman?

It is natural for children to want to do well and to feel bad when they do not. And it is good for children to learn how to apologize with sincerity: "I am sorry." "I made a mistake." "I was wrong." "Please forgive me." *We have to model the behavior we want to see in our children.* Parents are a child's natural heroes. If we yell at our children, become impatient or short with them, forget to do what we said we would do, it is vital that we look them in the eye and sincerely apologize. When we disconnect, we can reconnect. A heartfelt apology can do much to bridge any distance between us.

It is good for children to be able to identify with their heroes. As our child's heroes, we have to model the virtues and qualities we would want to see in our children. We have to be strong, fair, honest, and wise. We have to model empathy, generosity, loyalty, commitment, dependability, responsibility, optimism, warmth, understanding, and patience. We have to model respect for appropriate authority, such as police officers and teachers, and rules, such as traffic laws that help to keep us safe. We have to model respect for ourselves and others.

We have to model both cooperation and independent thinking. We are not mindless lemmings. We do not participate in lynching mobs. We are respectful to all people regardless of any superficial differences.

We regularly help others. We include our children in what we do while working with others. Include your child when you do Meals on Wheels, stack wood for an elderly neighbor, do grocery shopping for a shut-in, harvest and share surplus vegetables from your garden with the soup kitchen and share them with friends and neighbors, shovel snow off an elderly neighbor's walk. Community service can be organized, but it does not have to be formal. It can be helping your family, friends, and neighbors. Let your child learn how good it feels to help others.

Not only do we model helping others, but we also teach how to help ourselves. A vital gift you can give to your children is to model recognizing and asking for help when you need it. This takes trust and vulnerability. We cannot do it all alone. We all need help. Children who cannot trust to ask for help are at a disadvantage all their lives. They not only do not know *how to* ask for help, they may not know that asking for help is something one does. And instead of being tossed a lifeline, they will drown because no one knew they were in need. Being able to ask for help when small is another thread in the fabric of connection.

It can be good for children to be part of a spiritual community. You might want to join a synagogue or a church of your

faith. Find a community in which you feel comfortable and welcome. Hell-fire and brimstone are not good for children. But
most religions are founded on brotherly love, acknowledging
that we are our brother's keeper. Love and acceptance and other
adults to help watch over the well-being of your child are what
you are seeking for your child.

Being part of a greater whole can be good for children. It
reduces the risks of anonymity, which encourages a lack of
accountability. Belonging to a church can provide children with
more caring and responsible adults who help to keep them safe.
It can serve as a moral compass if necessary. And it can offer a
wholesome social life, which is something children and teens
need. A spiritual community in which all are there to help one
another is good for your child.

About gender differences: The core of both boys and girls is
love. There are similarities and differences. Generally, boys like
to tunnel in the mud, and girls like to make neat little pies. Boys
can sit on a curb and watch a construction sight for an hour.
Girls seldom do. Boys often like to roughhouse and, if they are
well adjusted, will do so good naturedly without malice. Girls
like to jump rope. Both like bike riding. It is important to honor
masculine and feminine differences.

It is good for both girls and boys to play house as mothers and
fathers caring for their children. Your children play-act parenting modeled on the mothering and fathering they have received
from you. Is your child rough and threatening? Is your child
gentle and caring? The doll is a neutral object receiving your
child's projections about parenting. You can learn a lot about
yourself as a parent during these moments. Children practicing
to be mothers and fathers is preparation for parenthood and is
to be encouraged.

A short story told to me by a mom: Her young son was having a birthday party. She had labored over the birthday cake, and
it was beautiful. A few friends had been invited to celebrate and

enjoy the cake and ice cream. The first to arrive were a mom and her three-year-old daughter. The three-year-old girl climbed up a chair and plunged her hand into the waiting cake, taking out a big chunk. The mother of the girl thought this was "cute." This was not cute. It is never okay to encourage children to believe that disrespect is cute. Watch your child and be aware of what she is doing when visiting. If something does happen, take responsibility, sincerely apologize and remedy the situation as best you can. Model respect for your child.

Charity begins with our own family, with our own children. Model the Golden Rule: We treat others the way we want to be treated. We live in light and love with others. This is the legacy we want to leave our children, grandchildren, great-grandchildren....

A great book you can read with your child is *50 AMERICAN HEROES Every Kid Should Meet* by Dennis Denenberg and Lorraine Roscoe. But remember the real-life heros are the parents we never hear about who quietly take care of their families.

Above all, our children are our priority. With every decision you make, ask yourself, "Is this good for my child? If not, then why am I doing it?"

We do our work the best we can. And we are kind. This is how we live.

Money Management

The price of anything is the amount of life you
exchange for it.
~Henry David Thoreau

Knowing how to manage your money responsibly is an important part of parenting. Children need parents who model how to use their money. This applies whether you are poor or affluent. Children learn how to avoid being victims of consumerism by your example.

Having enough money helps. Many of us will have enough money if we budget, buy only what we need, and live a healthy lifestyle. I believe people who have more than enough money have to model for their children how to be charitable with their wealth.

Budget for small emergencies such as a washing machine that breaks down unexpectedly. Try to save even if it is a small amount. It adds up.

Live within your means. *Do not spend money you do not have on things you do not need.* Remember the New England heritage of frugality: If money is tight, then use up what you have, wear it out, make it do, or do with out. Ask yourself these questions:

Do we need it?

Can we afford it?

Can we live without it?

BEWARE OF THE FASTEST GROWING RELIGION — CONSUMERISM!

Materialism does not bring happiness. Children do not need things. Beware of littering your children's minds, lives, and the Earth with cultural garbage. Beware of confusing needs with wants. *Why do you "want"?* Do you want things because you are trying to fill an empty space inside?

Children do need to be warm and clean, have durable, sensible, comfortable, and attractive clothing in classic styles, nutritious food, and a safe and pleasant home. A home can be both modest and nice.

Be sure to dress children appropriately and in good repair. Mittens, hats, scarves, boots and warm jackets in the winter. Clean underwear changed daily, including socks, underpants, undershirts. Shoes should provide support and fit properly. Children should look like children. It is disturbing to see a child in adult fashions.

No one needs beer, cigarettes, lottery tickets, SUVs, fashion designer clothes (every season), big houses, exotic vacations, or expensive toys. No child needs plastic toys, electronic toys, cell phones, video games, or any other gimmick corporate America can come up with to separate you from your money. Buying furniture or appliances on time is the most expensive way you can buy an item. If you would like something, save your money.

With your money held in hand, go to the store to buy what you need. Forget using credit cards.

Celebrate birthdays by giving your love lavishly and material items modestly. Try inviting a friend or two to visit the aquarium or planetarium, or go canoeing on a nearby pond, and return home for cake and ice cream. Stay connected by focusing on the person. Keep to one special gift, such as a subscription to a quality magazine (*Ranger Rick* or *Dig*, etc.) or a good book, and a few little things like a pencil and sharpener, a ball and jacks, a jump rope. (Please, no plastic toys, no battery operated anything, no video games or other electronic devices.)

A note about Chanukah and Christmas: These holidays are not a time to spend your last penny or go into debt. Religious and spiritual holidays are a time to gather together in celebration as family and community in gratitude and appreciation, to give what we can to others who are less fortunate, to enjoy making and listening to the rich legacy of traditional music, to delight in and share the wide variety of delicious ethnic and other festive foods, to decorate tastefully and naturally. Stay connected. Stay sane.

I know families who have found alternatives to excessive gift-exchanging. They give only what they have made or set a limit of spending at five dollars per gift or, for older family members, pull a name out of a hat and give one gift per member. Or they tell the children to write a list of two or three things they really would like and the parents will try to get them one. Some give only to others who have less than they do. Teach your children that Christmas or Chanukah is not for getting but for giving.

We have only one body, so we don't need much clothing. Classic styles made of natural fibers such as cotton work. Some folks take advantage of Goodwill or the Salvation Army for good buys in clothing. Don't waste your money on cheap plastic junk. Buying anything disposable usually adds up to be costly. If you need an appliance such as a washing machine, then it is a good idea to buy the best you can afford and take care of it so you can enjoy its service for a long time.

It is wonderful to have conveniences such as a refrigerator and stove, a washing machine and dryer (though fresh sheets dried outdoors are wonderful, too), a safe and reliable vehicle, central heating. These advantages may be viewed as reasonable and helpful. No one *needs* every gadget manufactured. Enough is plenty. It is best for your child to learn to *live simply* through your example.

Take advantage of free entertainment such as hiking and picnicking in state parks and the books, resources, and often free programs public libraries offer. It costs nothing to sing around the campfire or tell spooky tales. And if anyone can strum a guitar, all the better.

My heart goes out to you if you are a mother (or single father) who has to work. In a more enlightened society we would ensure that mothers and children are together. For other mothers, setting priorities, managing money, and being creative can enable you to be there for your child when she needs you. Mothers have always worked, but they have worked with their babies on their hips. Be creative. How about starting a small business from home? I know mothers who have a diaper washing business, do sewing and alterations, bake cakes and pies, do architectural design, write newspaper articles. One single mom does home healthcare for the elderly, taking her young daughter with her. When a child is at least three, work weekends while the kids stay with Dad. Have a family owned business where the children are with both of you. (This is even better! Children and dads miss each other too!) Work mother's hours. *And* have a live-in grandma.

No matter what the setup is, it is really hard to find the time and have the energy to give your children the attention they need if you work. There aren't enough hours in the day to do all that needs to be done for a family. You can't afford to stay home? Your can't afford *not* to stay home. Invest in your children when they are small. The return is beyond rubies.

We need little. We can live a rich life with little money. When we have food in the pantry, wood in the shed, and each other, we have what we need.

Nature

Children need nature. Nature is not a luxury. It calms the agitated and energizes the depressed, keeps us in harmony, delights the senses. Nature can be a spiritual connection. We are not apart from but rather a part of nature.

A true story: This story is not about children but adults who were in some ways child-like. Years ago I worked with folks who were mentally retarded. One day, my task was to take two folks to a nature park. Scott was subdued and nonverbal. He always wore a helmet to protect his head due to seizures. Sally suffered echolalia. She would relentlessly repeat a phrase. It was a perfect summer day. The moment Scott and Sally stepped out of the van they looked around and were transformed. A radiant smile lit up Scott's face. And Sally quieted! It was amazing to witness. For an hour, these two tortured souls felt peace and joy.

A word of caution about overwhelming your child with saving the world: It is too much too soon for a small child to feel responsible for saving the whales or the rain forests. First, let her feel the wonder of nature. Let your child feel as one with the natural beauty that surrounds her. If a child grows up feeling personally connected to the natural world, it is likely that she will live responsibly as a steward on Mother Earth and will not be clear-cutting and paving parking lots where wetlands, fields, and forests should reign. This is how a child will learn to care about her world.

Children need to feel the sun on their faces and the wind in their hair. Children need to ride bikes and play ball, build forts and climb trees, explore woods and streams, study anthills, collect and identify rocks, watch cloud formations, listen to the peepers heralding spring, see a rainbow after a summer thunder shower, experience geese flying overhead in a V against a brilliant blue autumn sky. *How do these wondrous winged creatures know when to migrate?*

The best place for a child who can't sit still is to be outdoors to run free in the fields and to explore the wilderness. To experience connection with nature offers comfort and transformation.

Children can also learn yard work such as mowing, raking, shoveling snow, weeding the garden. They can perform these tasks for elderly neighbors, learning how to care for others. Together, you and your child can pick up litter in your neighborhood, on the beach, or where you find it, as long as it is safe for you to do so. Caring for our neighbors, friends, and Mother Earth is an important part of how we live.

Children can benefit from working alongside us in the garden. Growing flowers and vegetables is a great way to help children learn how to nurture.

Garden projects are flourishing in many schools. Knowing how to grow vegetables can be an important life skill. These students learn hands-on about math, science, business, world trade, history, nutrition, and community. Living and working on a farm is the best education a child can have. Teach your child that farming is an honorable profession. Farm life also teaches a child about seasons and the life cycle.

Take a lot of walks with your child. You can make your walks a learning experience. You can go to the library and look at field guides to identify the flora and fauna you see and hear as you walk. Many folks like to be able to put a name and some background information to a flower, bird, or animal track. Or you can enjoy the simple pleasure of walking together, filled with conversation or just shared in companionable silence.

We are always learning, consciously or unconsciously. Learning does not have to be deliberate. And it is not always measurable. When your child is walking with you, she is learning that you care about her enough to give her your time, your life, which your child will perceive as love. Is there anything more important? You are creating a time and place for your child to be close to you.

Learn about the wonders of nature together. Read together about the work of naturalists such as John Muir and Rachel Carson.

You and your children might like these books about children and nature:

- *The Sense of Wonder* by Rachel Carson

- *Sharing Nature with Children: The Classic Parent's and Teacher's Awareness Guidebook* by Joseph Cornell

- *Roots, Shoots, Buckets and Boots: Gardening Together with Children* by Sharon Lovejoy

- *The Last Child in the Woods: Saving Our Children From Nature Deficit Disorder* by Richard Louv (adult)

- *The Geography of Childhood: Why Children Need Wild Places* by Gary Paul Nabhan and Stephen Trimble (adult)

- *The Giving Tree* by Shel Silverstein

Nutrition and Lifestyle

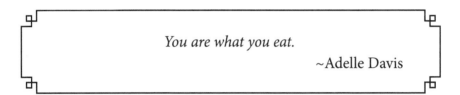

You are what you eat.

~Adelle Davis

Many common illnesses today are due to eating bad food and living unhealthy lifestyles. Take the example of obesity, which has become rampant across all ages. Until recently, few children were obese; now many are. This is disturbing and sad. I believe much of the childhood obesity we bear witness to is due to a hungry heart. Children are *starving* emotionally to feel a parent's love and approval, a void that no amount of food will ever fill. But overeating foods high in calories, low in nutrition, and loaded with questionable nonnutritive additives, coupled with a sedentary lifestyle, are major factors.

Mothers have to eat right before and when expecting and when nursing. Nursing your baby is natural. Breastmilk, exclusively, is best for infants under six months and continuing till both mother and child are ready to stop. Solid foods are best when introduced gradually usually at about six months of age, using only whole foods.

The only food in the house should be healthy food. Then children can eat what they want, and what they eat is not an issue. How much a child eats is a personal matter. Never insist that a child eat what he dose not like. How we taste is individual and personal. If an older child does not like dinner, then he can make himself a peanut butter sandwich.

Soda is bad for children. It is best that soda be reserved for special occasions such as a birthday party. Junk food should be occasional as well. Processed sugar is bad for children. Drinking juice is not the same as eating the whole fruit. Water is best. Unless allergic, milk, preferably certified organic milk, is good for children. Avoid anything that has artificial coloring, flavoring, preservatives, hormones.

Offer fresh fruit, vegetables, whole grain products, free range eggs and chicken, organic meats, natural cheese, etc. Organic is better. Eat close to the earth. Coops offer healthy choices in food. There is a lot of information out there about whole food.

No drugs. Unless you have a medical condition that cannot be corrected by living well, *don't take medication.* Legal or illegal, pills are not the answer to life's problems. The current drug culture (coupled with sedentary and emotionally detached technology) will be our undoing. A bottle of aspirin is all you need in the house.

No smoking. Secondary smoke is *bad* for your child, as is your example of smoking — in mind, body and spirit. A healthy animal does not foul its body or its nest. Be clean. Your young child will imitate you. It is good for your child to see you eat right, be active, and get the rest you need to be well.

Eat dinner together as a family. Set the table. No distractions. No phones, radios, TVs. Say a thanksgiving for good food and family. Share food and conversation about what happened to everyone that day and what is happening in the world. Children benefit from this ritual. They like the sense of order eating a prepared meal together provides. It is a comfort.

Included in a healthy lifestyle is hygiene. Children need to be clean. Traditional Native American Indians believed we should bathe twice daily and not to do so was unhealthy. It is good for children to learn how to brush their teeth. You have to show them how and be with them.

It is good for children to learn to wash their hands before eating and after they go to the bathroom. Children need clean clothes and fresh bed linens. Children need to live in a clean and orderly home. They can help work along side you to keep your home nice. The key is *alongside you*. Telling small children to go clean their room will prove to be a frustrating exercise for both of you. Work together side-by-side. Putting your house in order is good for your child to experience and learn from.

Possessions can be a burden. The less you own, the less you have to take care of, and the more time you have free to think, feel, do and just be.

A word about pets. For the first eight years of my life my dog followed me everywhere I went, and she was my best friend. Some parents believe pets with children is a given. They believe pets teach children about life cycles, which is true. Farm children learn naturally about birth and life and death. Living on a farm and being active in 4-H Club is every child's dream. A farm is set up to accommodate farm animals, and large dogs can run, and cats can catch mice. But to see a large dog tied up in a small yard seems sad to me.

Pets are messy, smelly, hairy, unsanitary, can spread disease, and be unpredictable. I know many instances where children have been harmed by pets. If you give pets the care they need and deserve, they will take time, energy and money. Caring for some pets, such as dogs, is like having another child. Having pets can add stress to an already too full day.

I strongly believe wild animals belong in the wild. They can take care of themselves much better than we can. My children and I went to a circus once. We cried when we saw the elephants manacled to a tree, their legs mutilated by the shackles. We would never go to a circus again. Nor a zoo. So, you decide about pets, but remember that you don't have to have pets if you find that they are more trouble than fun. If you want to care for a living thing, you might want to consider growing plants. The issue of neglect is less critical, and plants are more forgiving.

When you know *how to* live a healthy lifestyle you can decide that health is what you want for your family and you just do it. It is a matter-of-fact. This is how we live.

I believe home economics classes should be brought back into schools. Home economics classes taught not only sewing, cooking, and basic housekeeping skills also childcare and social skills. All would benefit. Kindergarten also can be devoted to learning social skills as kindergarten once was intended. These simple amendments to public education would be a step toward sanity.

Quality and Quantity Time

I want to emphasize the need for you to *be with* your child, to appreciate the significance of spending time with your child. You have to be visible and tangible for your child. Your child has to hear your voice, read your face, feel your energy, observe your behavior, and receive your direction.

You are hungry. You go into a restaurant and order steak of the finest quality. The waiter returns bringing you one cubic square inch of delicious steak. But one square inch of steak merely serves as a tease, leaving you hungry and wanting more. And so can a token of quality time. It is like feeding an elephant a blade of grass, resulting in either an elephant turned ugly or apathetic. It simply is not enough.

Your child cannot feel the warmth of your affection from a distance or in ten minutes of "quality" time. If something has to give, it should not be your child. Eliminate the other things from your life but never your child. Keep your life simple. Your child has to come first. Your child has to feel that he is special to you. Be crazy about your child and show it. Walk your talk: You can't say, "I love you!" and, in the next breath, turn around and walk away and expect your child to trust you. *Without trust you have less than nothing.*

"Quality time" is a myth. Life with children does not work that way. Often children need just your presence, your availability. Quality happens within a quantity of time. Too little quality time leaves your child always wanting for more of you, unsatisfied and frustrated. You and your child need a quantity of quality time to be together.

Please Read

> *You may have tangible wealth untold,*
> *Caskets of jewels and coffers of gold.*
> *Richer than I you can never be.*
> *I had a Mother who read to me.*
>
> ~Strickland Gillilan

Read often, every-day, to your child beginning before birth and continuing through adolescence. Reading is free. Reading is fun. Reading expands our world. Free public libraries are great places with which to become familiar. Reading builds vocabulary and listening skills. Children who can read well and enjoy reading have an advantage all of their lives. Human babies are born patterned to be creatures of words.

A high school English teacher told me that every year she asks her students who remembers being read to when they were little. Those who raise their hands are the students who do well.

As with anything else, forcing a child to read before she is ready does not work. If a child is surrounded by good and live books (live books are books that are authentic and come from the author's personal experience), it is likely that they will read and with pleasure.

Reading is rich! Memories can be made from reading together. A friend my age remembers her grandmother reading to her and her siblings Sunday afternoons from the Scribner classics with those wonderful N. C. Wyeth illustrations. These were the same books her grandmother read to my friend's mother. Alongside the paragraphs, in pencil, the grandmother carefully made notations of when she read and to which children. The link of sharing books between generations means so much my friend. She now works in a bookstore.

It is good for your child to see you reading. This is because your child wants to do and be just like you.

TV Is Bad for Children: The Tyranny of Technology

> *There is more to life than increasing its speed.*
>
> ~Mahatma Gandhi

TV is *so bad* for children for so many reasons. The *best* thing for most families is to have no TV in the home. This is because the tendency for abuse is high.

Both the content and context of TV is harmful. Research has proven that in current films, the images change too quickly for the human brain. And the content is often unethical and vulgar. Do you want this malevolent presence in your home? A home should be a sanctuary from evil. Would you invite someone into your home who talks like TV?

TV violates your child with violence and disrespect. TV contributes to the "violentization" of our children. The threat of desensitizing children and teaching them a violent mentality is greater for children who are at risk, but it is equally abusive to connected children. Why should anyone be repeatedly subjected to the offense of violence?

TV contributes to children's instability. Many children do not know who they are. They dress and behave like the characters they see on TV. They become confused about what is real and what is fantasy. The images they see burn into their psyches. Once seen, these images are not forgotten.

TV is used by corporate America to convince your child she is inadequate and sacrifices your child upon the altar of the idol of consumerism. Would you let your child drink a bottle of bleach? TV is just as toxic as bleach.

Watching TV is passive rather than interactive. Children need interaction to learn to be responsive. Watching TV teaches children to just stand there while someone is sad, hungry, bullied, dumps their groceries in the parking lot, is assaulted on a street corner. It never occurs to them to help pick up those groceries, to respond to a another's need. They may not even notice that there is a need. TV involves watching others do things. TV does not teach an attitude or mentality of doing. It teaches oblivion, indifference, apathy, incompetence. A lifelong pattern of disconnectedness has begun.

A nonprofit recently relocated its office to my local area. The entire family of Dad, Mom, and the children — two girls of about thirteen and ten and a boy of about six — all helped move the dad's office into the new space. These children are homeschooled and smart, well-behaved, friendly, and willing. A spirit of inclusiveness and cooperation prevails. TV never taught a child to work cheerfully. These children reflect their parents' behavior.

Until your child is about six years old, you have the power to control her environment. You decide what to expose her to and what she can explore. What your child listens to in the womb will determine what your child will respond to after birth. Good or bad, children tend to turn to that which is familiar. Only what we know exists.

Connected children often know best what their basic needs are, such as how much to eat or when they are tired and need to sleep. But children do not know how to protect themselves against cultural threats. Nature did not anticipate TV. Parents and all adults have the responsibility to be sensitive to images, ideas, and behaviors for which children are not ready, and to protect children from harmful exposure.

As far as we are able, we best fill a child's first few years of life with everything good and free of personal strife and strain. A secure base gives them a chance to build a reserve of inner strength from which to draw upon during rougher times. Childhood should be as golden as we can make it. Remember how flowers that have had a chance to grow strong roots can better withstand an assault. Seedlings are fragile. The late educator and child advocate John Holt said, "The best preparation for hard knocks is good knocks."

Some families have a TV but no cable, with only two channels, one of them public. Other families use only the VCR. One family I know watches a movie they borrow from the library once a week as a family, replete with hot buttered popcorn. Some homeschooling families use the TV to play instructional videos such as algebra or banjo videos.

Many children are becoming withdrawn, addicted to video games and other handheld electronic devices. They play these games while in the checkout line at the supermarket, in the car, at a restaurant. Video games are noted for their cruel and callous destruction, and some have warnings on the packages. Video games are bad for children.

Children do not need TV. Children do not need violent videos games that preclude thinking, feeling, interacting, living. Children need nature: fresh air, sunshine, and fun. They need physical activity and relationships with real people. Children need meaning in their lives.

Computers are better left alone till at least age twelve. Children have to learn to be connected to themselves, to others, and with the natural world before they become distracted by computers.

Cell phones are far more disconnecting than connecting. As with e-mail, there is no interpersonal connection. There is no commitment. People have to have the noise of portable media players so they cannot think or know what they feel. Noise "music," which many young people listen to on their portable media players, is dissonant, discordant, violent, abusive. Disconnecting technologies are bad for children.

Until about 1960 or so, we usually benefited from mechanization and new technology, which helped to take the wretched drudgery out of our everyday lives and make our lives more comfortable. And who would deny the benefits of a PET scan, CAT scan, or MRI rather than the knife? But I believe we have crossed over the line. I believe we now are regressing rather than progressing.

The more we become enamored with technology, the greater the risk that there will be no room left for humane thinking, feeling, and caring human beings. The abuse of modern technology is both a cause and effect of detachment. Just one example: We have to question intensive measures of keeping babies alive to baptize them in torture and pain when nature would have them embraced in peaceful death. There are things worse than death.

As parents you have the right, responsibility, and power to abolish the weapons of detachment from your developing child's life. No child needs TV, video games, portable media players, or cell phones. You and your children should be far too busy living life to watch other people play-acting on a TV screen or withdraw into a computer. TV is called the plug-in drug for a reason. Read a good book. Learn a new skill. Help someone.

Sing and dance. Learn how to play an instrument and start a family band. Make music! Beautiful music! *Not* heavy metal, violent rap, or worse yet, destructive noise "music," all of which cannot be classified as music and are bad for a child's developing brain. Listen to music that is good for the brain, such as works by Mozart. And the melodies and lyrics of the show tunes, big bands, traditional jazz, bluegrass, spirituals, lullabies, folk music, and other genres can be just fun or beautiful, inspirational, and uplifting.

With your child: Build something out of wood such as a birdhouse or the back steps; repair something that needs fixing, wash and wax the car, take a walk; plant a garden, learn a foreign language, learn sign language, knit a scarf, bake cookies, visit an elderly neighbor, write a book, paint a picture, start a parenting support group in which adults talk and children play or listen, clean your house, play chess or Candyland or checkers or Monopoly or cribbage, pick up litter or look for sea glass along the beach, volunteer for Meals-on-Wheels, join the 4-H Club, Brownies, or Cub Scouts, visit a museum, join a theater group, build a snowman or a sand castle, fly a kite, volunteer at the Humane Society, learn ballroom dancing, take photos and put together a family album. Do some good in the world.

Robert Louis Stevenson wrote, "The world is so full of a number of things that we all should be as happy as kings."

You will notice that many children appear to be in an altered state while watching TV and go haywire when it is turned off. What do you think about this observation? Eliminating TV from your family's life is one of the easiest steps you can take to help your child be healthy and happy. Eliminating TV is good for your child. And rather than costing you money, it will save you money.

Life is for living and giving, not being numbed by an electronic drug. Be mindful and responsible. Protect your child.

Beyond the First Decade

onnected teens are easy. All the destructive behaviors teens are commonly associated with are not an issue when teens are connected. *Connection is the issue.* It is unlikely that your teen will choose a destructive path if the affection connection with your child is strong. A strong affection connection is the best protection you can give your child against all the social ills that can befall a more vulnerable child. A family that eats and talks together, works together and plays together, stays together. Share a common interest. It works.

There need not be a "generation gap" between you and your adolescent child. Before, she went through the terrific twos; now, she has the years of *awesome adolescence*. If you and your child are connected, you will enjoy awesome adolescence just as you did the terrific twos. Drugs and alcohol, tobacco, promiscuity, theft, curfews and so on will not be an issue. They are never the issue. Connection is the inoculation. Your relationship with your child will protect her. Peers are more important than parents only when the parent/child relationship is weak. A child secure in your love will have little need to self-destruct.

In a parent/child relationship based on trust and affection, a teenager who knows security and freedom since birth does not require artificially imposed limits such as curfews. These children know who they are, and they know their natural limits. Rather than a relationship based on fear, power, and control, you have created a relationship based on mutual trust. There is nothing to oppose or go against. There is no need to protect oneself from being swallowed by another. What you want now is to create the least restrictive environment for your child as you have always done.

By your example as parents who are true to each other, and from the sensitive and open dialogues your family engages in, your teen will already understand about healthy boy-girl relationships.

It is natural for teenage girls to be thinking about boys and boys to be thinking about girls. They look forward to meeting their life partner with whom to share a family and home. This is normal. To be fulfilled, most of us need meaningful work and someone special with whom to share our experiences. A young adult who is comfortable with herself can learn to recognize another's intentions. Is that person operating from a place of fear or love? Does he feel secure or threatened? Is his intention an equalitarian relationship or one of power and control? Is he connected? Will he treat me with love and respect? Not only is he trustworthy, but can he trust? Can he be intimate? These are some of the questions to ask one's self about another before involvement and commitment.

As I grow older and somewhat wiser, I am inclined to believe that we can avoid causing much unnecessary grief for ourselves and those around us when we value the sacredness and exclusiveness of a deep and committed relationship between a couple. Our intentions have to be honorable before we become more than friends. And certainly, being friends comes first. Rather than dating we might return to the old-fashioned but perhaps not-out-of style practice of courting.

In their program, Great Aspirations, Doug Hall and Russ Quaglia have identified eight principles that build upon the other, resulting in confident, competent, happy, motivated persons. They are belonging, heroes, a sense of accomplishment, fun and excitement, curiosity and creativity, spirit of adventure, leadership and responsibility, and the confidence to take action. I believe these steps lend themselves to a connected teen who can blossom: a person who can be fully actualized. This is successful parenting.

As in every relationship, remember the Law of Attraction: Negative attracts negative, and positive attracts positive. What you focus on is what you get. Likely, your growing child will meet your expectations and behave as well as he is treated.

A hint: Be sure to take family photos of your children and yourself. You can write who, what, when, and where on the back of the pictures. This visual history of your family will be cherished for generations to come. Become an oral historian of your family. Make audio recordings of memories of grandparents, aunts, and uncles. These family stories are fascinating to younger generations. Precious deeply personal memories are dying everyday. Capture them when you can.

Conclusion

It is the fate of every truth to be an object of ridicule when first acclaimed. It was once considered foolish to suppose that black men were really human beings and ought to be treated as such. What was once foolish has now become a recognized truth.

~Albert Schweitzer

Human beings are born to love and to learn. We have to give expression of our love. When this expression is thwarted we become ill. The diagnosis is disconnection.

Emotional connection is necessary to prevent detachment. Unless a child is emotionally connected, nothing else matters. Your influence with your child is only as strong as your relationship.

Connected children are so rare in our society that many people have no experience of what a secure child can be like. This includes researchers who manufacture data and statistics. Much research and data are flawed because few research subjects are normal. How can research conducted with diseased children project healthy conclusions? If you want health you have to study health.

I wish I could convey the delight in being with a child who has had his needs met: to be close to his mother, to feel her unconditional love and affection, and to have a strong and gentle father who provides for and protects him, who makes him feel loved and lovable. Such a child is pure joy.

The first step we have to take is to ensure that every child has his birthright to mothering honored. Then we have to value fathering and ensure that fathers are present and available. And we have to follow the continuum of connection with each age and stage of development.

Resonance means to vibrate with. When each one of us resonates with the other we are on the same frequency range. We create order out of chaos. In a state of resonance we are free to take pleasure, to be joyful, to be generous. In a world of resonance, there are no prisons, no police, no war. Imagine such a world.

The most urgent task of our time is the choice between connection or disconnection. To be connected or not to be connected is *really*, "To be or not to be?" To choose life or death (suicide). To care or not to care. To feel or not to feel. To fear or not to fear. To love or not to love. Everything we do we do because of love. In the end, love is the only thing that matters. But we do have to learn *how to* express our *will* to love.

The greatest threat to national security is not external but internal. We are our own worst enemy. WAR children, children who are raised in a World of Abnormal Rearing, only know how to make WAR. To be disconnected is the only life they know. We learn what we live, and then we live what we have learned. And disconnection is a life of unmitigated misery. WAR is insane.

What your child wants most in all the world is to be close to you. And you to them.

There is nothing stopping us but our own fear, the fear that we are not good enough to be happy. But our true self IS good. Look at a tiny baby. Could that precious, innocent child be bad? *It is absurd to believe that a newborn baby is bad.* The notion that we are born bad is wrong. What makes any of us so different from that of a newborn baby? We are all children. We are all innocent. I wonder how much unnecessary pain the notion that children are inherently bad has caused throughout the history of humankind. To be happy is our normal, natural, healthy, and right state. You and your child need, want, and deserve to be happy.

The problem and solution are one. Maternal deprivation and paternal deprivation compounded by an insane world are the problem. First mothering and then fathering are the solution: nourishment and education. To feel loved and lovable and to learn how to live are essential needs naturally met while growing up in a loving and caring family.

When your children are first, and you are secure and possess basic parenting skills, raising connected children is simple and easy. It is the other stuff — work, money, housing, food, clothes, media, and other people — which is hard. It would be helpful if public policy and community would encourage mothers who stay at home with their young children and fathers who bear the burden of supporting their families. But we do not have to wait for government systems to catch up to speed.

Like-minded folks are finding each other and working together to raise their families. Moms and tots get together and visit, and while they visit, the kids play with each other, and the moms share ideas and friendship. They swap clothes and surplus food from their gardens and form a great networking partnership. I believe this is the way we will effect the most positive change. One family helping another and, in turn, another and yet another. Good will beget good.

Mothering does come first. How can it be otherwise? Look at the proximity of relationship for the first nine months of a baby's life. Can you get any closer? It is the mother who carries, gives birth, and nurses her baby. It is the mother with her surging hormones who is wholly focused on her infant for a year or longer after the birth. If this is the only thing you learn from reading this book, know that a newborn or young child is lost in body, mind, and soul without his mother. *Nature requires nurturing*. And mothers nurture. This is not negotiable. I know men who have that gift of nurturing. They are extraordinary. My son, a very manly man, exercises sensitivity and intuition with his son like that of a mother. I wonder, if, in a sane society, these extraordinary men would become more ordinary. But typically, women are Mother/Earth, and men are Father/Sky, nurturer and teacher.

Ninety-year-old men who are dying call for their mother. A woman who has lived nearly a hundred years on this earth lost her mother to tuberculosis when she was four years old. "I have missed her ever since," she told me with tears in her eyes. Mother and child are linked forever.

Self-examination and insight into our behavior is important because it allows us the possibility of interrupting negative/anti-life cycles and replacing them with positive/pro-life ones, leaving our children with a healthier and happier legacy to pass on for generations to come.

Nature bats last. *And nature requires nurturing.* When we raise our children according to the Laws of Ecology, our children will grow secure in the knowledge that they are loved and will have learned how to love as a direct effect of having experienced our love. Concurrently, these children will know how to live, as well. These children are the hope for yet another generation of connected children. These children who know what goodness is will change the world by being who they are.

Your thoughts produce your feelings; your feelings direct your actions and often the reactions of others. Think about what you want for your children and grandchildren. Think about how you want living in this world to be. You have the power to prevent the unnecessary suffering from Parent Deficit Disorder. It is easy with your good enough parenting.

Love and bring forth your children.

APPENDICES

Diseases of Nonattachment

Signs and Symptoms of *Parent Deficit Disorder*

Frederick Leboyer wrote in poetic language about birth and its traces, which are "everywhere . . . in all our human folly, in our madness, our tortures, our prisons, our legends, epics and in myths."

The primary bond and a continuum of healthy attachment a child and mother share can help to prevent many emotional, mental, social, and physical ills, aided by the father's important role as the infant grows into child and adult. When a mother cannot, due to absence as in the case of illness, a father may assume the major role in attachment between parent and child.

Detachment (disconnection) is a permanent state of Post Traumatic Stress Disorder (PTSD), often as a result of separation of mother and child compounded by absent fathers and an adversarial society. The following is a partial list of the diseases of nonattachment that the practice of organic or attachment parenting helps to protect children against. I discuss several in depth in the pages that follow.

> Parent/Nurture Deficit Disorder (a cycle of cause and effect)
> Professional Anxiety
> Postpartum Depression
> Bullying
> Domestic violence and child abuse
> Pornography
> Sexualization of our children
> Shaken Baby Syndrome (SBS)
> Sudden Infant Death Syndrome (SIDS)
> Accidents
> Failure to Thrive (Marasmas)

Divorce

Family dysfunction

Depression (sometimes a lifetime of depression with no identifiable cause)

Suicide

Low self-esteem

Stealing

Infidelity

Prostitution

Promiscuity

Drug dealing

Rape and predatory stalking

Pedophilia

Murder and serial killing

Prisons

Psychopathy

Addictions to alcohol and other drugs

Cutting, tattooing, piercing

Obesity

ODD/ADHD/ADD/DDD

If the trauma of separation leaves a child's brain in a permanent state of PTSD or reactive chaos: Might these chaotic behaviors be a reflection of that internal state of disorder the origin of which can be found in infancy?

In General: Detachment expressed as a self-destructive and destructive personality. I believe detachment contributes to most emotional and/or mental illness and much physical illness, such as cancer, colitis and heart disease, to name a few.

The Problem of Professional Anxiety

The problem of professional anxiety is pervasive in our systems, including social services and education, which have become big business with the dollar as the bottom line. Professionals such as doctors, nurses, childcare providers, teachers, and anyone working with families and children are susceptible to this sign and symptom of detachment.

The problem of professional anxiety is to be overwhelmed with pain, leaving one shut down and feeling no pain at all. Awareness of the problem of professional anxiety can allow professionals to be vigilant and to take precautions to protect themselves from this detachment.

Postpartum Depression

Connected parenting helps protect mothers against postpartum depression. Just as for newborns, the biological expectation of a new mother is to hold her baby close to her heart. I believe postpartum depression would be rare if our cultural expectation was compatible with nature, for mother and child to remain as one; if mothers and mothering were valued and honored; if we ensured that mothers and children were together.

Bullying

Bullying has always been a problem in society, but it appears to be increasing. I believe part of the problem is that what once was understood as wrong and taboo is now viewed as "cool." "As long as you can get away with it" is becoming an attitude translated into lifestyle. This attitude is a symptom of a detached society.

Bullying is not what it appears to be on the surface. Bullying comes under the law of paradoxes. A child who has been made to feel powerless seeks power over others. Bullies are terrified. Power and control become everything.

What can we do about bullying in schools or neighborhoods? Make it a clear and open public policy that bullying is mean and unacceptable. If we witness bullying, we will join together to interrupt the bullying and to support the victim. We will not do this by attacking the bully but by telling the bully that he is better than that. He does not need to bully.

The bully may or may not be able to hear kind words. It is the nature of the disconnected to be disconnected. They will not let you near them to help. We can explain bullying, but we cannot excuse it. We do not have to allow a bully to hurt us. Children should report bullying incidents to adults. There will be no secrecy. And there will be follow-up. We are strong and protected when working together. We might be able to protect the bully from himself or from the demons that drive him to destruction.

Domestic Abuse

Domestic abuse is a result of the separation of mother and child, plus a pattern of violence. A child who has not satisfied his need for healthy attachment with his mother also cannot complete healthy separation. The dynamic between mother and adult child, and then between adult child and significant other, become twisted. How sad and perverse to have to link love with pain. *How do we reconcile fearing that which we most want?*

Most often, children are expected to believe that their abuse is normal, that they deserve it, and that they should "just take it." There will be no protest. Adults who recognize that they did not deserve to be mistreated may be able to break the vicious cycle of abuse. But it is too painful for some adults to face their abuse as children and to admit that their parents betrayed them. This creates a climate of emotional dishonesty. To be vulnerable is anathema. Their hearts are *hard* and unyielding. These men have become the "hard guys" Dr. James Kimmel wrote about in his brilliant book, *Whatever Happened to Mother?* (gals can be hard guys, too).

Have you ever been with a person who changes moods from light to dark and sometimes back again in an instant?

Encountering this Dr. Jekyll and Mr. Hyde behavior leaves us feeling crazy. Mr. Hyde has been associated with alcoholism and drug abuse. PTSD also involves surging mood-altering chemicals manufactured by one's own body.

Control has become the dominating force in the lives of such tormented persons who torture others. Such a person operates from the primitive part of the brain that deals with survival. The primal, or reptilian brain, will *react* to the situation as it perceives it must in order to survive. This is why a spouse can be enraged with a partner and appear to be calm and in control when the police officer arrives. The enraged spouse is not in control; the primitive brain is in control. And the primitive brain believes it must manipulate all to protect its existence. The innate and essential *trust* we are born with has been extinguished.

Yet, with every person the adult child meets, but especially with a significant other, he is still searching for what he should have had but never did — two logs that burn as one — that first year together of unconditional and seamless love. This is when a mother anticipates her infant's needs before he knows he has them. No words are necessary. Love and approval are a given. A child cannot move on emotionally without experiencing this perfect love, possible only when held in-arms during a child's first year after birth. His frustrated need for mother's love and approval has become like a leaky pail that never can be filled.

The tragedy of domestic violence has little to do with anger management, as many working in the social service field would have us believe. Instead, it is the primal scream of an abandoned child caught in a relentless vortex of anguish for all.

The subject of domestic violence is a complicated one and requires its own book. Domestic violence *is* preventable.

Normative Sexual Abuse of Children: The Epidemic of Pornography and the Sexualization of Children

The proliferation of pornographic materials cannot be ignored. We should be terribly concerned about our children's exposure to the dehumanizing effects of pornography. How is pornography shaping our children's values and attitudes? I believe pornographic images are traumatic to children, leaving them confused and damaged. Pornography is a multibillion-dollar industry without conscience. Obscenity is not a First Amendment right. Parents and other adults have to speak out against this evil. Our silence is evil.

Sex without reverence is madness. Sex changes everything. Sexuality as a physical expression of love between two adults who are committed to and care about each other is healthy. Adult sex involving children has to be a taboo. The disregard of the taboo of combining sex and children is one of the gravest indications of our cultural decadence.

We can dress our children in clothing that is appropriate for children. We can give them toys that encourage natural expression (baby dolls, not Barbie dolls). We can keep our homes free of the anti-humanity of detached sex and instead fill it with genuine love and affection. We can also be vigilant and vocal about putting the well-being of children before greed.

We should speak honestly with our children if they should ask about our position against certain clothing or TV programs or toys. We can speak in simple age-appropriate language and a sincere manner. We can differentiate between healthy sex as an expression of caring and unhealthy sex that is exploitative. And we can model the role of healthy adults safeguarding vulnerable children.

Childhood is sacred.

Shaken Baby Syndrome (SBS) and Sudden Infant Death Syndrome (SIDS)

As a mother, your presence alone helps to protect your child from illnesses such as Shaken Baby Syndrome (SBS) and Sudden Infant Death Syndrome (SIDS).

Most SBS occurs in reaction to a baby's crying inconsolably in the absence of his mother. Only his mother can comfort him. And the perpetrator will do anything to stop that intolerable crying. Not only would a baby not have to cry for his mother if she were with him, but also the attempt to shake a baby would be less likely. In the event that the attempt was made, many mothers would intercede, with fierce protective force if necessary. Few biological mothers are perpetrators.

In the case of SIDS, a newborn depends upon her mother to help her regulate her respiratory and circulatory (heart) systems. Resonance like this can happen only when mother and child are physically and emotionally close. A child and mother are a unit, are one at birth. Kangaroo care, when a baby is held close to her mother's heart, is good protection for all babies.

Accidents

Accidents can be prevented by a parent's presence. An attuned mother knows what her young child is up to. She keeps a watchful eye and a listening ear . She can intercede to keep her active, curious child safe. Also, children who enjoy a secure attachment seem to have a sixth sense about what is safe. They seem to sense what they can and cannot do, and can exercise intuitive judgment as to risk-taking.

There Is More

Many folks who practice connected parenting are conscious and conscientious about living a healthy lifestyle. They tend to eat well, are physically active, and get the rest they need. They make wiser choices. Obesity, stress, high blood pressure, tooth decay and diabetes are affected by one's personal health habits.

Connected parenting helps to create connected children. And for children who feel connected, the following are not an issue: escaping by way of constant noise (always being plugged in so they can turn off), which makes it impossible to think or feel (connection to self); bullying (feeling powerless); gangs (trying to meet their need for belonging); stealing (desperately and futilely attempting to give themselves something important, an intangible, that they feel they do not have, with a tangible); drugs (dulling the pain); cutting (distracting attention from intolerable emotional pain and anxiety with external pain); suicide (the final solution to a temporary problem); smoking and numbing addictions (linked to past trauma and a sense of alienation) such as alcohol and other self-destructive and aggressive behaviors against others. *The issue is connection.* It is all the same.

For most children (and many adults if they can be reached at all) who are suffering from mental illness and physical illnesses caused by emotional pain, the therapy they need is mothering. *Nature requires nurturing.* The alienated need a mama to give them what they never got: availability 24/7 and unconditional love. It takes some knowing to combine meeting those dependency needs with the added needs of other ages and stages. Mothering naturally includes the discipline of learning how to live.

These are just a few ills that connected parenting helps to protect children against. Can you think of others? Raising children by the Three R's of respect, responsibility, and reverence makes good sense.

Divorce

Broken vows always mean broken hearts.

Why do you want a divorce?

Rampant divorce is both cause and effect of a society mired in clay. But in many cases divorce can be preventable.

A retired middle school teacher told me this story. One year, the students in her class were outstanding. They were every teacher's dream. They were polite, cooperative, confident, competent, enthusiastic, intelligent, creative, sincere, and caring.

The students two years later were the opposite of those in the dream class. School that year was a nightmare. Going to school was not fun for anyone that year.

Administration and instructors tried to understand why. What made the difference? They concluded that the great majority of the children who were in the dream class came from two-parent homes. The majority of students in the miserable class came from single-parent homes.

If a parent is sexually abusive, take your child and leave *now*. Sexual abuse is the worst. Physical and emotional abuse hurt and harm our children. Be honest with yourself about that proverbial stinking elephant who is sitting in the middle of your living room. Children have to be protected by all caring adults from all abusive adults. Children have to feel safe and secure. Most children will choose peace over a raging alcoholic.

But if a parent is not abusive, then most children will want to be with their natural mother and natural father together in a loving and caring family. Children know this arrangement is best for them. Unless a parent is abusive, it is within the best interests of your child to remain together and treat each other with kindness and respect. Once you have children, you have given up the right to divorce.

Children do not do well in the fractured families of divorced homes. I have never met a well-adapted child from a divorced home. Usually, children who appear to be adjusted have detached. Many children suffer arrested development. The experiment of the single-parent home is not working.

This is important: In their pain, children often feel responsible and guilty for their parent's division. If you divorce, be sure to communicate clearly to your children that they are not the reason for your fractured family. Assure them of your love for them and of their innocence.

A few women I know who have lost a spouse or were unable to avoid divorce have devoted their lives to their children till their children were eighteen. They did not want to be preoccupied with a romantic relationship at the expense of their children. And to invite an outsider inside could not fill the void left by an absent father. Several of these mothers joined households with the children's grandparents making the load they had to carry as single mothers much lighter. These wise women are good models to emulate.

Do you believe people are disposable or interchangeable? We all have idiosyncrasies. As long as a difference is not illegal, hurtful to any living thing, immoral, or unethical we can be tolerant. These are character traits. Every family has members who are characters. And they can make life more colorful.

Put the well-being of the other parent of your child above your own. Take care of that person. You want to do what is best for your child. An intact family is best for your child. You can choose to be happy. And if the other person cannot be kind, you can anyway. The only person you can control is yourself.

Never use ugly language about your child's other parent to your child. Never fight each other in front of your child. Would a good counselor help?

Before you separate, ask yourself, "Why do I want a divorce?" Do you want a *divorce,* or is it something else? Are you actually reacting to unfinished business from your past? If the reason you want a divorce is something other than abuse, can you work something out? It may be hard. Most marriages involve a lot of effort.

Practically, how will you survive with resources of money, time, and energy being divided or diminished? And when a child has one parent, she often has no parent. Distracted parents are unavailable both physically and emotionally. And the absent parent misses his child every hour of his life.

Stepparents and stepparenting bring a whole host of other problems. And rather than leaving your problems behind, you likely will experience the same problems but with a different person.

I have met many divorced parents who regret a divorce a few months after but have no mechanism to return. Too much has happened to go back, and they do not know how. They are not happier. Neither are the children.

For all your differences, you share one overriding commonality with the other parent of your child: your child. Can you reconcile your differences? If both of you always make decisions based upon what is best for your child, then divorce is not a consideration. Honor your family's need for connection.

Geese are true and loyal to their mates for life. That's the way it should be. Stay together and be good to each other.

Reconnection

I and the public know
What all schoolchildren learn:
Those to whom evil is done
Do evil in return.

~W. H. Auden
September 1, 1939

This is a book about prevention and health, not intervention and disease. There are many others who are working from an intervention perspective. But I will say a word or two about reconnection.

When we lack essential nutrients we show signs of deprivation. We become ill. So it makes sense to give an ill person what he lacks so he may get well. Mothering or nurturing is the therapy most people need, followed by fathering. Time, attention, unconditional love, and approval, and then life skills. Learning how to do the right thing the right way. They need the connection of belonging. Of *family*.

If a child lacks a critical nutrient in early development, such as Vitamin D or calcium and her bones grow deformed, it is unlikely that we can make up for that loss when a child is twenty. A child may learn to compensate, but the deformity may be permanent. A woman who works at a greenhouse and also cares for houseplants in her own home told me if a too thirsty plant is greatly stressed, there is no recovery. Children are like flowers.

For the disconnected, the crucial issue of trust is tenuous. An older child or adult may respond positively to a person who takes a sincere interest in him as long as that person appears to accept him unconditionally. But dominating fear lies just under the skin, and any perceived or actual rejection will quickly be felt as a betrayal.

The bank account of trust is full for the newborn. He is programmed to trust his mother and expects her to be trustworthy. Every time she fails to honor that trust, a little is withdrawn from the account, but there might be enough left in the account from which to draw. The trust account of a detached person has been long overdrawn, and the account is closed. He is left with an empty cupboard. And an empty cupboard cannot give. There may be dust, spider webs, mildew, and debris in that cupboard, leaving these folks operating with a negative. Their expectation is to be disappointed. They cannot separate what they do or say from who they are. For example, they cannot tolerate threatening disagreement. Once again, as the infant who was separated from his mother, he feels terrifyingly alone. Now, he is one against the world.

Detachment is due to trauma and poor parenting. Trauma can be due to reasons that are not directly related to parenting. The death or critical illness of a mother, babies who experience a difficult birth, and babies who are premature or suffer birth defects that require intensive care can predetermine detachment. Neonatal Intensive Care Units are traumatic for an infant. An infant needs her mother most is when she has her least. In these cases, while an infant is always bonded to her mother, she cannot become securely attached.

Rehabilitation really is *habilitation*. Disconnection can also happen further along the continuum. A four-year-old who suddenly loses his mother or an eight-year-old whose parents divorce may suffer detachment as well, though differently than a newborn. Twelve-year-old boys are painfully sensitive to their parents' divorce.

Before birth, most babies are connected. If a birth is gentle and a baby is welcomed, she will remain connected, and by nature (biology), expect that connection to continue in the arms of her mother. When we disappoint them, when we interrupt the natural continuum of healthy attachment, infants react by disconnecting or detaching. The sheer terror of being separated from their other self, their mother, catapults infants' or young children's brain into a state of chemical chaos that can be permanent. The disorganized and insecure thinking and behavior we are witnessing in our young people and society today is a reflection of and reaction to — a direct result of that primal wound. Children, and later adults, who have suffered the shock of separation are unable to form healthy relationships. How can we repair the damage?

A china dish cracks in two. With careful and skillful attention we might be able to glue the dish together again. The crack will always be there. But the dish remains a dish and is functional. The beauty may be marred, but that crack is part of its history and tells a story. Each one of us has a story. Many stories.

If the dish is shattered, it may be impossible to put it back together. Reconnection is unlikely. A shattered dish should be the rare exception to a set of whole and intact dishes. We can endure a chip or two, but there is a limit beyond which there is no repair.

Helping people spiral upward takes much time, energy, and attention. It takes relationships, one-on-one. It takes trust. People who are not well-nourished or well-educated cannot be expected to have the same values as those who are. Many cannot read well. The written word matters hardly at all; the spoken word matters little without matching action. What you *do* matters. Head, heart, and hands working together. You cannot appeal to their intellect because folks preoccupied with survival operate from the reptilian brain, or reactive brain.

People who have lived through a childhood without parental love and guidance are chronologically adults, but emotionally they are more like motherless children. They are big feral children. You have to reach their heart and mind, if you can. First, folks have to feel *safe*. Then maybe they can listen and feel if they aren't too dead inside, but entrenched patterns of behavior tend to endure. The prognosis for detached people is poor.

I recently met a woman in the grocery store who was buying shrimp for her eighteen-year-old cat. The woman had found and befriended a feral mother cat and her two feral kittens eighteen years earlier. Even now, after eighteen years, this elderly cat has a timid relationship with the woman who has been so committed to her care. And unable to trust, she remains distant from every other human.

Based upon my experience, the only possible and decent way *very young* children — under the age of five — who are detached might be helped is by *recreating the primal relationship*. You have to go a child's point of need and start from there. Though zig-zagging and overlapping, development is sequential — with one stage building upon the successful completion of the previous. You have to start where development stopped. And for a four-year-old, this could mean responding to the needs of a newborn. This involves far more of our inner resources than most folks are willing or able to give. Once understood, it is a simple therapy, but not easy for most people to follow through on. And I do not know of many counselors who understand attachment and are willing to provide the support that would be necessary for this type of therapy. You might do it yourself without a professional counselor, but you have to be connected, and it helps to have family and community support.

There is no cure for detached adults. Like polio victims, we become lame for life. Sometimes, due to age, a life crisis, or being just plain tired of "living" a crazy life, people will decide to change their behavior. But I think the change is from the out-side in. It's behavioral. They are still detached and terribly alone. Usually, they do not act out their detachment anymore. They no longer beat their wives, rob banks, or engage in prostitution. But during times of great stress, they tend to regress or revert to their old patterns of behavior and coping mechanisms. Typically, they dissociate, self-sabotaging with the violent reactions of PTSD. It is not that they do not want to be close. It is that they can't. It's the best they can do. They are no better than they should be.

Detachment can manifest from the quiet desperation of a poor soul who cannot give expression to her deepest yearnings; to the man who pays charming attention to other women while ignoring his wife; to the partial psychopath of Wall-Street who is driven to acquire power, prestige, and money; to the psychopathic serial rapist-killer who make up the walking dead. Those on the extreme negative end of the attachment-detachment continuum might find themselves incarcerated. Our prisons are filled with detached men and, increasingly detached women.

Again, the prognosis for detachment is poor. We have to do right by our children the first time because there is no second chance.

Prevention of deadly detachment with good enough parenting is the only solution I know that works.

Adoption

We have not talked about adoption. If it is at all possible, it is within the best interests for a baby to remain with her natural mother. A newborn's natural expectation is to continue to be with the one she has been with for nine months, her mother. It is imperative to understand that mother and child are one, emotionally, at birth.

Some people would like to believe that infants are unknowing and unfeeling when the truth is that they are highly sensitive little beings. They are fragile human seedlings. A separated infant will grieve for what she did not have and the source of the separation cannot be identified. This is the primal wound.

I know great folks who have taken sad and sometimes horrifically neglected and abused children into their hearts and homes, and given them love and a far better life than they would otherwise have had.

A baby boy who suffered extreme neglect was rescued at seven weeks and now is four years old. His mother heartfeltly told me that their family is "so blessed." Every night, as the family holds hands around the dinner table, this little boy insists upon saying, "Thank you for my mommy, thank you for my daddy, thank you for my sister, Amy." The positive energy of this family is evident. These are very honest and exceptional parents with an extremely hands-on dad.

But love might not be enough for issues that adopted (and foster) children might have. Some additional insights and concrete know-how may be helpful. A sensitive therapist who understands attachment-detachment issues may be helpful in working with an adopted child and family. Family therapy is not exclusive to families with adopted children who might suffer detachment. Many families can learn new parenting and life skills and become more functional. As individuals, we are always a part of a family system. All therapy or counseling has to be built on a foundation of compassion.

Warning! There is a movement afoot to inflict a perverted therapy upon attachment disordered children called holding therapy. *Holding therapy in an attempt to treat reactive attachment disorder is abusive.* In holding therapy, a child is held forcibly against his will. Sometimes the child is not released until he makes eye-contact. The intent is to take away the child's free will, resulting in compliance and submission. This is for the child's "own good." the same justification as has been used for spanking and other punishments. As Dr. Alice Miller wrote, "A more perfect deception and distortion of someone's perceptions is barely imaginable."

Rarely, we might briefly hold an out-of-control child firmly yet gently in our arms *to protect* that child, or *to protect* another child who has become the target of a child's physical assault. Rarely and briefly. And only by someone who genuinely loves and cares about the child. Attachment parenting is based on trust. Forcibly holding a child is a mockery of this trust. Arms are for holding, lovingly.

Never let anyone violate your child by imposing holding "therapy" upon him.

Model Child-protective Legislation

Melanie Killen, Professor of Human Development and Associate Director of the Center for children, Relationships, and Culture at the University of Maryland, proposed the following legislation in Project NoSpank. Let it be implemented.

1. No child shall be subjected to cruel, degrading, or humiliating treatment.

2. No child shall be corporal punished or otherwise subjected to the deliberate infliction of physical pain as a means of control or for reasons of punishment.

3. No child shall be deliberately denied the fulfillment of his or her fundamental bodily needs, including but not limited to the need for:

   a. nourishment
   b. rest
   c. warmth
   d. cleanliness
   e. movement
   f. waste elimination
   g. essential medical care

And my addition:

4. No child shall be denied his or her inherent right to appropriate nurturing to develop the capacities for trust, empathy, and affection that are the central core of what it means to be human. No child will be denied his or her *right to mothering*.

Cowardice asks the question: Is it safe?
Expediency asks the question: Is it politic?
Vanity asks the question: Is it popular?

But conscience asks the question: Is it right? And there comes a time when one must take a position that is neither safe, nor politic, nor popular — but one must take it because it's right.

~Martin Luther King Jr.

Parenting Education Quotes

There are a thousand hacking at the branches of evil to one who is striking at the root.

~Henry David Thoreau

I have been encouraging the Maine Department of Education to include *attachment* parenting education in public schools, beginning with kindergarten, offering parallel programs to parents. Waiting to teach parenting in high school is far too late.

In public schools, a gardening program can be a great low-risk way to begin learning how to care for a living thing. Each child could have her own plant, such as a geranium in the classroom, and eventually take it home. Perhaps a greenhouse could be erected and used throughout the year, with seedlings started and then transplanted in the outdoor garden. Programs would be organized according to climate and pocketbook. But raising a few plants need not be expensive. And nature is healing.

Nurturing is the most important lesson a human being can learn.

This is the most important job we have to do as humans and as citizens. If we can offer classes in auto mechanics and civics, why not parenting?

~Alvin Poussaint, M. D.
Professor, Harvard Medical School
Author of *Raising Black Children*

The development of a child does not begin the day he is born — or at the age of three — but much earlier, during the formative years of his parents.

~Edward Zigler, Ph.D.
Sterling Professor of Psychology and Director
Bush Center in Child Development and Social Policy
Yale University

Why do we require training and a license to drive a car but have so little regard for preparing students to be parents, workers or family and community members? These skills are not innate and should be taught k-12 and not as an add-on or elective. Life is the final exam.

~Marilyn Swierk,
Chair
Elementary, Secondary, and Adult Education Section
American Association of Family and Consumer Sciences

The way a society functions is a reflection of the childrearing practices of that society. Today, we reap what we have sown. Despite the well-documented critical nature of early life experiences, we dedicate few resources to this time of life. We do not educate our children about development, parenting or about the impact of neglect and trauma on children. As a society we put more value on requiring hours of formal training to drive a car than we do on any formal training in childrearing.

~Bruce D. Perry, M. D., Ph. D.
Professor of Child Psychiatry,
Baylor College of Medicine
and Chief of Psychiatry, Texas Children's Hospital;
John Marcellus, M. D.
Scholastic.com (2000)

[A] child who is not nurtured is a child who never learns to trust, never develops empathy, never accepts responsibility for his behavior, and hurts others with impunity.

~Barbara T. Kelley, Terence P. Thornberry, Ph.D.
Carolyn A. Smith, Ph.D.
"In the Wake of Childhood Maltreatment"
Office of Juvenile Justice and Delinquency Prevention
U. S. Department of Justice, August, 1997

Morality comes from empathy, the ability to understand another person's feelings and to care about how he or she feels. And empathy is developed through nurturing interactions with caregivers and parents . . . Children who don't get this nurturing are likely to be two or three steps behind, no matter how hard we try to help them catch up.

~Dr. T. Berry Brazelton
Professor Emeritus, Harvard Medical School
Dr. Stanley Greenspan
Clinical Professor of Pediatrics and Psychiatry
George Washington University School of Medicine
"Our Window to the Future" in "Your Child"
Newsweek, Special Edition (Fall/Winter 2000)

Because of parenting education there has been an increased sensitivity to the needs of infants and others. There has been an increased understanding of dependency upon others for various needs.

~Parenting education teacher
Frances M. McKay School, Chicago Public Schools

For over twelve years I have implored governors, legislators, boards and directors of education to implement a Parenting Curriculum in the school system . . . As a family court judge for almost ten years, I cannot count the number of times that children come before me unaware that the physical and/or sexual abuse they were suffering at home was not the norm.

~The Honorable Benjamin J. F. Cruz
Chief Justice of Guam
The 1999 State of Judiciary Address
A Report to the People of Guam

Despite public rhetoric promoting a "prevention model" of wellness, American society continues to operate primarily in a "crisis intervention mode." Public education could serve to improve the quality of life for individuals, family and community members by helping students acquire the knowledge and skills needed to function successfully in their current and future adult roles.

~Barbara A. Woods
Consultant, Family and Consumer Sciences,
Vermont Department of Education

NURTURING: The single most important skill to acquire during the process of growing up. Children and teens who are capable of nurturing themselves, others and their environment can relate in a positive way to society. We all benefit.

~Stephen J. Bavolek, Ph.D.
Founder and President
Family Development Resources

It is the responsibility of every adult — especially parents, educators, and religious leaders — to make sure that children hear what we have learned from the lessons of life, and to hear over and over that we love them and that they are not alone.

> ~Marian Wright Edelman
> *The Measure of Our Success*
> Founder and President
> Children's Defense Fund (CDF)

ADDITIONAL RESOURCES

BOOKS

Below is a list of just a few books I recommend. If you want more recommendations, or are interested in a specific topic, please feel free to call me.

- *RAISING OUR CHILDREN, RAISING OURSELVES*
  Naomi Aldort

- *ECOLOGY*
  Ernest Callenbach

- *Early Childcare: Infants and Nations at Risk*
  Dr. Peter Cook

- *The Day Care Decision*
  Wendy and William Dreskin

- *Raising Boys: Why Boys are Different — And How to Help Them Become Happy and Well-Balanced Men*
  Steve Biddulph

- *Every Child's Birthright: In Defense of Mothering*
- *The Magic Years*
  Selma Fraiberg

- *The Natural Child: Parenting from the Heart*
  Jan Hunt

- *Whatever Happened to Mother? — A Primer for Those Who Care About Children*
  James Kimmel

- *High Risk: Children without a Conscience*
  Dr. Ken Magid and Carole A. McKelvey

- *Ghosts from the Nursery: Tracing the Roots of Violence*
  Robin Karr-Morse and Meredith S. Wiley

- *The Womanly Art of Breastfeeding*
  La Leche League International

- *Birth without Violence*
  Frederick Leboyer

- *The Continuum Concept*
  Jean Liedloff

- *Make Way for Ducklings*
  Robert McCloskey

- *The Elephant Man*
  Ashley Montague

- *The Scientification of Love*
  Michel Odent

- *Natural Family Living: The Mothering Magazine Guide
  to Parenting*
  Peggy O'Mara

- *Beyond the Rainbow Bridge: Nurturing Our Children from Birth
  to Seven*
  Barbara Patterson and Pamela Bradley

- *Separation and the Very Young*
  James and Joyce Robertson

- *Our Babies, Our Selves: How Biology and Culture Shape the Way
  We Parent*
  Meredith Small

- *The Native American Book of LIFE*
  White Deer of Autumn

- *The Velveteen Rabbit*
  Margery Williams

Any other books by the above authors are also recommended. Other authors you might want to check out on specific topics are:

Advocacy

Alice Miller

Attachment Parenting

Elliott Barker
Robert Karen
Joseph Chilton Pearce
Karen Walant

Babies

William Sears and Martha Sears

Birth

Sheila Kitzinger

Learning

John Taylor Gatto
John Holt
Alfie Kohn

Living with Children

Sidney Craig
Thomas Gordon
Adele Faber and Elaine Mazlish

Sleep

William Sears
Tine Thevenin

MAGAZINE

Mothering
Phone: 1 800-984-8116
P. O. Box 1690
Santa Fe, New Mexico 87504

ORGANIZATION

La Leche League International
Phone: 847-579-7730
1400 N. Meacham Road
Schaumburg, Illinois 60173-4808

WEB SITES

- Aware Parenting Institute - Aletha Solter
  www.awareparenting.com

- The Liedloff Continuum Network - Jean Liedloff
  www.continuum-concept.org

- Empathic Parenting - Elliott Barker
  www.empathicparenting.org

- Natural Child Project - Jan Hunt
  www.naturalchild.org

- Daycares Don't Care
  www.daycaresdontcare.org

MOVIE

- **Into the Wild** — 2007 film based on 1996 non-fiction book of same title written by author Jon Krakauer